DIY Fame

Navigating the Entertainment Industry
Without a Publicist

Ebonie Caldwell

First edition 2024

Contents

Chapter One

Introduction to DIY Fame

Understanding the New Landscape of the Entertainment Industry

The entertainment industry has undergone a significant transformation in recent years, driven largely by advancements in technology and shifts in consumer behavior. Musicians, filmmakers, influencers, and content creators now find themselves navigating a landscape that is more democratized than ever, allowing for greater access to audiences but also presenting new challenges in visibility and competition. Understanding this evolving landscape is crucial for those looking to establish their presence and achieve success without the traditional support of a publicist.

One of the most notable changes is the rise of digital platforms, which have become central to how entertainment is consumed and promoted. Streaming services, social media, and video-sharing platforms have shifted the focus from traditional media outlets to direct engagement with audiences. This means that artists and creators must not only produce high-quality content but also develop savvy digital marketing strategies to ensure their work reaches the intended viewers. The importance of building a personal brand online cannot be overstated; it is often the key differentiator in a crowded marketplace.

Social media, in particular, has transformed the way artists and influencers interact with their fans. Platforms like Instagram, TikTok, and YouTube offer unique opportunities for creators to showcase their work, share their stories, and engage with their audience in real-time. For musicians, this has led to innovative approaches to music promotion, such as viral challenges and behind- the-scenes content that can resonate with viewers on a personal level. Understanding how to leverage these platforms effectively is vital for creating a loyal fanbase and driving engagement.

The entertainment industry has dramatically evolved over the last decade, driven primarily by technological advancements and the proliferation of digital platforms. Traditional barriers to entry, once guarded by agents, publicists, and media moguls, have become less formidable. The rise of social media, video-sharing platforms, and music streaming services has empowered creators to bypass these gatekeepers and independently build their careers. Today, anyone with a smartphone, an internet connection, and a creative spark has the potential to reach millions globally. This shift has democratized fame, allowing individuals to cultivate their audience and brand without the need for a traditional publicist or major industry backing.

Navigating this new landscape requires a different skill set than what was needed in the past. Talent, while still crucial, must now be paired with a keen understanding of digital marketing, content creation, and community engagement. DIY fame is as much about strategy as it is about creativity. Artists need to become their own publicists, mastering the art of self-promotion across various platforms. This involves regularly producing high- quality content that resonates with their target audience, building a personal brand that stands out, and engaging with fans in an authentic way. The ability to understand and utilize social media algorithms, SEO strategies, and digital advertising tools is essential for gaining visibility and expanding one's reach.

One of the most significant advantages of the DIY approach is the autonomy it offers. Without the constraints imposed by traditional industry structures, creators have complete control over their image, messaging, and career trajectory. This freedom allows for more experimentation, enabling artists to explore different creative directions, connect with niche audiences, and adapt their brand in real-time. The direct relationship with their audience also allows for immediate feedback, which can be invaluable for refining their craft and growing their brand. Moreover, this independence means creators are not beholden to the demands or expectations of publicists or industry executives, which can often stifle artistic freedom.

The rise of platforms like YouTube, TikTok, Instagram, and Spotify has created a fertile ground for DIY fame. These platforms allow creators to distribute their work directly to their audience without needing intermediaries. YouTube, for example, has launched the careers of numerous musicians, comedians, and influencers, offering them a platform to showcase their talents to a global audience.

Similarly, TikTok's algorithm-driven content discovery system has made it possible for users to go viral overnight, with many creators leveraging this fame to build sustainable careers. Instagram, with its focus on visual content and personal branding, has become a vital tool for influencers and artists looking to connect with their audience on a more personal level.

Monetization is another area where DIY fame can thrive. Creators now have multiple revenue streams available to them, from ad revenue on platforms like YouTube to sponsorship deals, merchandise sales, and crowdfunding. Patreon, for example, allows creators to earn a steady income by offering exclusive content to paying subscribers. This direct-to-fan model not only gives creators more control over their financial situation but also strengthens their relationship with their audience.

The ability to monetize without relying on traditional media outlets or industry gatekeepers is one of the most empowering aspects of the DIY fame model.

However, the DIY path is not without its challenges. Without the backing of a publicist, creators must wear many hats, often juggling content creation, marketing, brand management, and business negotiations on their own. This can be overwhelming, particularly for those who are new to the industry or who lack experience in these areas. The pressure to constantly produce content and stay relevant in a fast-paced digital world can lead to burnout. Moreover, the algorithms that drive platforms like Instagram and YouTube are constantly changing, meaning that creators must stay informed and adaptable to maintain their visibility.

Another challenge is breaking through the noise in an increasingly crowded market. With so many creators vying for attention, standing out can be difficult. This is where branding becomes crucial. Successful DIY fame requires a strong, unique personal brand that resonates with an audience. Whether it's a distinctive visual style, a unique voice, or a compelling narrative, having a clear and consistent brand identity can help creators differentiate themselves from the competition. Building a loyal fanbase also takes time and dedication.

Consistency is key – both in terms of content output and engagement with followers. Creators who are able to build a community around their work are more likely to succeed in the long term.

The lack of industry connections is another hurdle for DIY creators. Without a publicist to facilitate media coverage, secure interviews, or arrange partnerships, gaining mainstream recognition can be more challenging.

However, there are ways to mitigate this. Networking with other creators, collaborating on projects, and attending industry events can help build connections that can open doors. Additionally, learning the basics of public relations, such as how to pitch to media outlets or negotiate partnerships, can be valuable skills for a DIY creator.

In this new landscape, success often hinges on the ability to balance creativity with business acumen. Creators must not only focus on producing great content but also on building a sustainable career. This means thinking strategically about how to grow their audience, diversify their revenue streams, and protect their brand. While the DIY approach offers more freedom, it also requires more responsibility. Creators must be willing to invest time in learning about marketing, branding, and business management if they want to succeed in the long run.

Ultimately, DIY fame in the entertainment industry is about taking control of your career and creating opportunities for yourself. It requires a blend of creativity, perseverance, and strategic thinking. For those who are willing to put in the work, the rewards can be substantial. The entertainment industry is no longer solely in the hands of a few gatekeepers – it's now an open field where anyone with the right mix of talent and hustle can thrive. Navigating this landscape without a publicist is challenging, but for many creators, it's also empowering. By leveraging the tools and platforms available today, DIY fame is not just possible – it's increasingly becoming the new norm.

In addition to social media, collaborations and partnerships have become essential strategies for gaining visibility. Celebrity endorsements can provide significant boosts to an artist's profile, while influencer marketing can help indie films and music projects reach niche audiences. Navigating these partnerships requires a keen understanding of branding and market positioning, as aligning with the right partner can amplify an artist's message and increase their reach exponentially. Creators must evaluate potential partnerships carefully, ensuring that they align with their brand values and resonate with their audience.

Finally, the importance of audience engagement tactics cannot be overlooked. As streaming platforms and digital media continue to dominate the entertainment landscape, creators must prioritize building relationships with their audience through interactive content, live performances, and personalized experiences. This engagement fosters a sense of community and loyalty, making fans more likely to support projects through merchandise purchases or attendance at events. By understanding the new dynamics of audience interaction, creators can cultivate a thriving and sustainable career in an increasingly competitive industry.

The Importance of Self-Publicity

Self-publicity is a crucial aspect of building a successful career in the entertainment industry, particularly for musicians, artists, filmmakers, influencers, and content creators. Unlike traditional publicity methods that often rely on hired professionals, self-publicity puts the power of promotion directly into your hands. This approach not only enhances your visibility but also fosters a deeper connection with your audience. As the landscape of media evolves, mastering the art of self-publicity can significantly impact your branding and marketing strategies, allowing you to stand out in a crowded marketplace.

One of the primary benefits of self-publicity is the control it provides over your narrative. By managing your own publicity, you can shape how you are perceived by your audience and the media. This autonomy allows you to highlight your unique qualities, artistic vision, and personal story, creating a compelling brand identity. In an age where authenticity resonates with fans, being your own publicist gives you the opportunity to communicate directly with your audience, fostering loyalty and engagement. Whether through social media, blogs, or personal websites, the ability to share your journey and milestones can create a powerful connection that traditional publicity may not achieve.

Furthermore, self-publicity enables you to be responsive and agile in your marketing efforts. The entertainment industry is fast-paced, with trends and audience preferences shifting rapidly. By taking charge of your publicity, you can quickly adapt your strategies to capitalize on current events, social media trends, or viral moments. This immediacy can be particularly beneficial for filmmakers and content creators who need to promote their projects in real-time, such as during film festivals or premieres. Utilizing platforms like Instagram, TikTok, or YouTube allows for immediate engagement, ensuring that your message reaches your audience when it matters most.

In addition to enhancing your personal brand, self- publicity can also open doors for collaborations and partnerships with other creators and brands. When you actively promote your work and showcase your unique style, you attract the attention of potential sponsors, collaborators, and influencers who align with your vision. This can lead to celebrity endorsements, brand integrations, and event marketing opportunities that would otherwise require a publicist's intervention. By establishing yourself as a proactive and engaging public figure, you increase your chances of being noticed and sought after in the competitive entertainment landscape.

Finally, self-publicity is a cost-effective strategy for those navigating the entertainment industry on a budget.

Hiring a publicist can be expensive, and not all artists or creators have the resources for such services. By learning the basics of self-promotion, you can save money while still effectively marketing your work. Investing time in understanding digital marketing strategies, audience engagement tactics, and content creation can yield significant returns, making your efforts worthwhile. In the end, mastering self-publicity not only empowers you as an artist but also positions you to thrive in an ever-evolving industry.

Who This Book Is For

The subchapter "Who This Book Is For" is designed to illuminate the diverse range of creative professionals who will benefit from the insights and strategies shared in "DIY Fame: Navigating the Entertainment Industry Without a Publicist." This book is tailored for musicians seeking to amplify their presence in an increasingly crowded market, artists aiming to carve out a unique identity, filmmakers hoping to connect with audiences, influencers looking to leverage their platforms, and content creators eager to build their brand. Each of these groups faces unique challenges in promoting their work and establishing a lasting impact, making the practical advice offered here essential.

Musicians and bands often find themselves in a competitive landscape where standing out is paramount. This book provides actionable strategies for building a recognizable brand, engaging with fans, and navigating the complexities of digital marketing specific to the music industry. By exploring case studies and proven techniques, musicians can enhance their visibility and create opportunities for celebrity endorsements and partnerships that can elevate their careers.

Understanding the nuances of merchandise branding also allows artists to diversify their income streams while further solidifying their brand identity.

For filmmakers and content creators, the stakes are high when it comes to marketing within the entertainment industry. The book delves into event marketing tactics for movie premieres and festivals, offering insights on how to create buzz and attract attention to indie films. It also emphasizes the importance of effective social media strategies for film and TV promotions, ensuring that creators can maximize their reach and engagement. By employing these tactics, filmmakers can effectively tell their stories and connect with potential audiences, all while maintaining control over their narratives.

Influencers and digital content creators are increasingly pivotal in shaping public perception and driving trends. This book equips them with the tools necessary to develop authentic partnerships and collaborations that resonate with their audiences. It also addresses influencer marketing strategies specific to the music industry, enabling creators to harness their influence effectively. By understanding audience engagement tactics for streaming platforms, influencers can create compelling content that captivates viewers and fosters community, leading to sustained growth and visibility.

Lastly, this book is a resource for professionals involved in branding and marketing across various entertainment niches, including brand integration in film and television and digital marketing strategies for indie projects. It provides a comprehensive overview of the essential tactics required to thrive in today's rapidly evolving landscape. By focusing on content marketing for entertainment news and reviews, readers will learn how to position themselves as authorities within their fields, ensuring that their voices resonate amidst the noise of the industry. "DIY Fame" is not just a guide; it's a roadmap for any creative professional determined to make their mark without relying on traditional publicist pathways.

Chapter Two

Establishing Your Brand

Defining Your Unique Identity

Defining your unique identity is a critical step in establishing yourself within the entertainment industry. In a landscape teeming with talent, having a clear and distinctive identity not only sets you apart but also serves as the foundation for your branding and marketing efforts. Whether you are a musician, filmmaker, influencer, or content creator, understanding who you are and what you stand for will guide your creative choices and inform your interactions with your audience. This chapter will explore practical strategies to help you articulate your unique identity, ensuring that it resonates across various platforms and mediums.

To begin, self-reflection is key in uncovering your unique identity. Take the time to analyze your influences, personal experiences, and artistic aspirations. What themes recur in your work? What passions drive your creativity? By answering these questions, you will begin to form a clearer picture of your core values and artistic vision. This introspective process not only helps you identify what makes you unique but also provides a narrative that can be communicated to your audience. This narrative becomes the backbone of your branding, allowing you to share your story authentically and connect with your followers on a deeper level.

Once you have a solid understanding of your identity, it's essential to translate that into a cohesive brand. This involves creating a visual and verbal language that reflects your unique traits. Consider your logo, color palette, and typography, as these elements contribute to your overall aesthetic. Additionally, your messaging should consistently convey your values and artistic vision. Whether through social media posts, interviews, or promotional materials, maintaining a consistent brand voice reinforces your identity and enhances audience recognition. This cohesiveness is particularly important when you engage with various marketing strategies, such as influencer partnerships or event promotions, as it ensures that your identity remains clear and compelling across different platforms.

Audience engagement is another crucial aspect of defining your unique identity. Understanding your target demographic and how they relate to your work will help you tailor your communication and interactions. Utilize analytics tools to gather insights about your audience's preferences and behaviors. Craft content that resonates with them, whether through behind-the-scenes glimpses, personal anecdotes, or interactive opportunities such as Q&A sessions. Engaging your audience not only reinforces your identity but also fosters a community around your work, encouraging loyalty and support that can be invaluable in the competitive entertainment landscape.

Finally, remember that your unique identity is not static; it can evolve as you grow as an artist and as the industry changes. Stay attuned to shifts in your creative journey and the broader cultural context. Adaptability is essential for maintaining relevance, but ensure that any changes still align with the core values and vision that define you. Periodically reassessing your identity will not only help you stay authentic but also keep your audience engaged and invested in your evolution. By grounding your identity in both self-awareness and adaptability, you will be well-equipped to navigate the complexities of the entertainment industry without relying solely on external representation.

Crafting a Compelling Brand Story

Crafting a compelling brand story is essential for anyone looking to carve out a niche in the competitive world of entertainment. A brand story serves as the narrative thread that connects you with your audience, making your artistry relatable and memorable. For musicians, filmmakers, influencers, and content creators, the ability to articulate your unique journey can set you apart in a crowded marketplace. This narrative helps to establish an emotional connection, allowing fans and followers to see not just the work you produce, but the person behind it. It's about showcasing your values, experiences, and aspirations in a way that resonates with your audience.

To begin crafting your brand story, introspection is key. Reflect on your origins, your inspirations, and the challenges you've faced along the way. This is where authenticity plays a crucial role. Audiences today are savvy and can quickly detect insincerity. Share your struggles, triumphs, and moments of vulnerability—these elements humanize you and make your story relatable.

Whether you're an indie filmmaker navigating the complexities of production or a musician trying to break into the mainstream, these experiences can serve as powerful anchors in your narrative. Remember, your brand story should not only tell who you are but also invite others to join you on your journey.

Once you have identified the core components of your story, it's time to refine and structure it. A compelling brand story typically follows a classic narrative arc: a beginning that introduces the protagonist (you), a middle that presents challenges, and a resolution that highlights growth and achievement. This structure not only makes your story more engaging but also allows for a clear message that can be easily communicated across various platforms. Adapt your story for different media— whether it's a short bio for social media, a more in-depth narrative for your website, or a pitch for potential collaborations. Each version should maintain the essence of your story while tailored to suit the context and audience.

In today's digital age, your brand story extends beyond text; it must be visually and audibly compelling as well. Utilize multimedia elements to enhance your narrative— videos, photos, and music can all serve as powerful storytelling tools. For instance, a behind-the-scenes video showcasing your creative process can provide insight into your artistic journey, while a documentary-style film can delve deeper into your background. These elements not only capture attention but also reinforce your brand identity, allowing followers to engage with your story on multiple levels. Think of ways to integrate your story into your social media strategy, ensuring that each post aligns with the overarching narrative you wish to convey.

Finally, remember that a brand story is not static; it evolves as you grow and change as an artist. Engage with your audience by sharing updates, milestones, and new challenges in your artistic journey. Encourage interaction and feedback, allowing your audience to feel part of your story. This ongoing dialogue fosters a deeper connection and loyalty among your fans. As you navigate the entertainment industry, keep in mind that your brand story is a living testament to your artistry, one that can inspire others while driving your career forward. By investing time and thought into crafting and sharing your narrative, you position yourself not just as a creator, but as a brand that resonates in the hearts and minds of your audience.

Visual Branding: Logos, Colors, and Aesthetics

Visual branding is a critical component in establishing a strong identity in the entertainment industry. For musicians, artists, filmmakers, influencers, and content creators, a cohesive visual identity can set the stage for successful marketing and audience engagement. At the heart of visual branding are three key elements: logos, colors, and overall aesthetics. These components not only differentiate an individual or project from competitors but also create an emotional connection with the audience, making them memorable and relatable.

Logos serve as the face of a brand. A well-designed logo encapsulates the essence of an artist or project, conveying messages about style, genre, and personality. For musicians, a logo might reflect the energy of their music, while filmmakers might opt for a design that hints at the themes of their films. The process of creating a logo should involve thoughtful consideration of the target audience and the core values of the brand. A logo should be versatile enough to work across various platforms, from album covers and movie posters to social media profiles and merchandise.

Colors play a pivotal role in visual branding as well. Each color evokes specific emotions and associations, which can significantly influence how an audience perceives a brand. For example, vibrant colors may suggest excitement and creativity, while muted tones can convey sophistication and seriousness. Understanding color theory can help artists and creators choose a palette that aligns with their artistic vision and resonates with their intended audience. Consistency in color usage across all branding materials reinforces brand recognition, making it easier for fans to identify and connect with the creator's work.

Aesthetics encompass the overall visual style and design choices that reflect an artist's or creator's unique voice. This includes typography, imagery, and the overall layout of branding materials. An effective aesthetic strategy should be tailored to the specific niche and audience. For instance, a content creator focusing on lifestyle and beauty may adopt a clean, minimalist aesthetic, while a hip-hop artist might opt for bold, dynamic visuals that reflect urban culture. By maintaining a consistent aesthetic, creators can build a recognizable brand that resonates with their audience and fosters a sense of loyalty.

In the competitive landscape of the entertainment industry, visual branding is not merely an option; it is a necessity. An effective visual identity can enhance marketing initiatives, improve audience engagement, and create opportunities for partnerships and endorsements. As musicians, artists, filmmakers, influencers, and content creators navigate their careers, investing time and effort into developing a strong visual brand can pay significant dividends. By thoughtfully combining logos, colors, and aesthetics, they can cultivate a lasting presence that captures attention and inspires connection in an ever-evolving digital landscape.

25 Tips for Establishing Your Brand in the Entertainment Industry and Why They Matter

1. **Define Your Unique Value Proposition (UVP)**
   Identifying what makes you stand out from others is crucial. Whether it's your personality, talent, or perspective, having a clear UVP helps you attract and retain a dedicated audience that resonates with your uniqueness.

2. **Develop a Consistent Visual Identity**
   Your logo, color palette, and overall aesthetic should be consistent across all platforms. This visual cohesion helps your audience immediately recognize your content, making your brand more memorable and professional.

3. **Be Authentic**
   Authenticity builds trust with your audience. People are more likely to connect with someone who is genuine and relatable rather than a carefully crafted persona that feels fake. Authenticity fosters loyalty, which is vital for brand longevity.

4. **Create High-Quality Content**
   Quality content is key to establishing yourself as a credible and professional brand. Whether it's videos, music, or social media

posts, delivering consistently high-quality content shows that you take your craft seriously and respect your audience's time.

5. **Leverage Social Media**
Social media platforms are powerful tools for building your brand. They allow you to connect directly with your audience, promote your work, and grow your fan base. Understanding the nuances of each platform can help you tailor your content and engagement strategies effectively.

6. **Engage with Your Audience**
Interacting with your fans creates a sense of community around your brand. Responding to comments, hosting live sessions, and acknowledging your audience's support makes them feel valued, which increases their loyalty and investment in your success.

7. **Collaborate with Others**
Collaborations expose you to new audiences and bring fresh perspectives to your brand. Working with other creators can also lead to creative breakthroughs and increased visibility, helping you expand your reach in the industry.

8. **Be Consistent**
Consistency in content production, branding, and messaging helps build trust and keeps your audience engaged. Regular content releases keep your brand top of mind for your followers and establish you as a reliable source of entertainment.

9. **Network Actively**
Building relationships with others in the industry can open doors to new opportunities. Attend industry events, engage with peers on social media, and seek out mentors who can offer guidance and introduce you to key players in the field.

10. **Master Storytelling**
Whether you're a musician, actor, or content creator, storytelling is at the heart of great entertainment. Developing strong story-

telling skills helps you connect emotionally with your audience and keeps them coming back for more.

11. **Stay Current with Trends**
Being aware of the latest trends allows you to stay relevant in a fast-paced industry. Incorporating trending topics or formats into your content can boost your visibility and show that your brand is in tune with the current cultural zeitgeist.

12. **Invest in Professional Development**
Continuously improving your skills keeps your brand evolving and competitive. Taking classes, attending workshops, and staying updated on industry best practices will ensure your talent and knowledge remain sharp.

13. **Be Strategic with Partnerships**
Choose partnerships that align with your brand values and resonate with your audience. Collaborations or sponsorships should enhance your brand, not dilute it. This keeps your messaging cohesive and maintains your brand's integrity.

14. **Create a Website**
Having a professional website acts as your digital headquarters. It allows you to showcase your portfolio, host your content, and provide a central point for fans, collaborators, and potential clients to learn more about you.

15. **Use Analytics to Guide Decisions**
Analytics tools on platforms like Instagram, YouTube, and TikTok offer valuable insights into what content resonates most with your audience. Use this data to inform your content strategy and make informed decisions that drive growth.

16. **Protect Your Brand Legally**
Trademark your name and logo, secure copyrights for your work, and consider legal protection for any unique content you create. This ensures that your brand is safeguarded from potential in-

fringement and maintains its uniqueness.

17. Embrace Your Niche

Don't try to appeal to everyone. Focus on a specific niche where you can become a leading voice. Narrowing your focus allows you to cater to a dedicated audience that appreciates your specialized content, leading to stronger connections and long-term loyalty.

18. Diversify Your Content

While consistency is important, diversifying your content across multiple formats (videos, blogs, podcasts, etc.) and platforms can help you reach new audiences and keep your current fans engaged.

19. Create Value for Your Audience

Your content should provide value, whether it's through entertainment, education, or inspiration. Valuable content fosters a deeper connection with your audience, encouraging them to return for more and share your work with others.

20. Develop a Personal Brand Voice

Your voice, whether serious, humorous, or inspirational, should be consistent and reflective of your brand's personality. A distinct voice makes your brand recognizable and helps you connect emotionally with your audience.

21. Build a Strong Portfolio

Showcase your best work across different mediums to demonstrate your versatility and talent. A strong portfolio not only impresses your audience but also attracts potential collaborators, agents, and sponsors.

22. Monetize Strategically

Choose monetization methods that align with your brand values and don't compromise your content's integrity. Whether it's through merchandise, Patreon, or brand partnerships, ensure that the ways you make money resonate with your audience and feel authentic.

23. **Plan for Longevity**

Building a sustainable brand requires thinking long-term. Plan for growth, anticipate industry shifts, and diversify your revenue streams to ensure your brand can evolve and thrive over time.

24. **Stay Authentic Under Pressure**

The pressure to conform to industry trends or others' expectations can be overwhelming, but staying true to your vision and values will ultimately strengthen your brand. Authenticity builds trust, which is invaluable for long-term success.

25. **Keep Your Passion Alive**

Passion is the driving force behind any successful brand. Continually remind yourself why you started and stay connected to what excites you about your craft. Passion not only fuels your creativity but also resonates with your audience, who can sense your genuine enthusiasm.

These 25 tips help build a solid foundation for your brand within the entertainment industry by combining creative vision, strategic planning, and audience engagement. With a strong, authentic, and consistent presence, you can navigate the complexities of the industry while cultivating lasting relationships with your audience and collaborators.

Chapter Three

Marketing Fundamentals

Understanding Your Target Audience

Understanding your target audience is a crucial first step in navigating the entertainment industry without a publicist. Whether you are a musician, filmmaker, influencer, or content creator, having a clear grasp of who your audience is will enable you to tailor your messaging, marketing strategies, and creative outputs effectively. The entertainment landscape is crowded, and with the rise of independent creators, distinguishing your voice and connecting with the right audience can make all the difference in achieving success.

To accurately identify your target audience, consider demographic factors such as age, gender, location, and income level. However, demographics alone do not paint a complete picture. Psychographics—understanding the interests, values, lifestyle choices, and behaviors of your audience—play a vital role in shaping your approach. For instance, if you are a musician targeting young adults passionate about social causes, your branding and messaging should reflect these values. Conducting surveys, analyzing social media interactions, and studying industry trends can help you gather valuable insights into what resonates with your potential fans or consumers.

Once you have a clear understanding of your audience, you can create tailored content that engages them on a deeper level. This involves developing a unique voice and aesthetic that aligns with their preferences. For filmmakers and content creators, this could mean producing behind-the-scenes content, interviews, or interactive experiences that allow fans to connect with your work. Musicians might benefit from sharing personal stories or insights about their creative process, fostering a sense of intimacy and authenticity. The more personalized the content, the more likely you are to cultivate a loyal following.

In the realm of social media, knowing your audience allows you to choose the right platforms and strategies for engagement. Different demographics gravitate toward different social media channels; for example, younger audiences may favor platforms like TikTok and Instagram, while older generations might be more active on Facebook. By strategically placing your content where your audience spends their time, you increase the likelihood of effective engagement. Understanding their online behaviors, such as peak activity times and preferred content formats, can further enhance your outreach efforts.

Lastly, audience engagement is not a one-time effort but an ongoing relationship. Regularly soliciting feedback, monitoring analytics, and adapting your strategies based on audience responses will help you stay relevant. Utilize tools to track engagement metrics and audience growth, allowing you to refine your approach continuously. By establishing a genuine connection with your audience, you not only enhance your brand's visibility but also create a community of supporters who are invested in your journey, ultimately helping you navigate the entertainment industry with greater confidence and success.

The Four Ps of Marketing: Product, Price, Place, Promotion

The Four Ps of Marketing—Product, Price, Place, and Promotion—serve as fundamental pillars in crafting effective marketing strategies, particularly within the entertainment industry. For musicians, filmmakers, influencers, and other content creators, understanding and applying these concepts can significantly enhance visibility and engagement, ultimately leading to greater success. Each component plays a crucial role in shaping how an artist or a project is perceived, making it essential to approach them thoughtfully and strategically.

The first P, Product, refers to the core offering that creators present to their audience. In the entertainment industry, the product can vary widely—from an album or a film to a digital course or a live performance. It is vital to define what makes your product unique and how it resonates with your target audience. This involves not only the quality of the content but also its positioning within the market. For instance, musicians should consider their genre, style, and the emotional connection they create through their music. Filmmakers might focus on the narrative, visuals, and the overall experience their film provides. Clearly defining your product helps in establishing a strong brand identity that can attract and retain an audience.

Price, the second P, encompasses the cost associated with the product. Setting the right price point is crucial, as it influences perceived value and accessibility. Creators must consider various factors, including production costs, market demand, and competitor pricing. In the case of independent musicians and filmmakers, pricing strategies could include tiered pricing for merchandise or ticket sales, subscription models for exclusive content, or pay- what-you-want systems for digital downloads. It's important to balance profitability with audience accessibility, ensuring that your offerings are enticing without undercutting your value or alienating potential fans.

Place, the third P, involves the channels through which your product is distributed and promoted. In today's digital landscape, this can encompass an array of platforms—from streaming services and social media to physical venues and online marketplaces. For content creators, leveraging multiple distribution channels can significantly increase reach. For example, a musician might release their album on Spotify while simultaneously promoting it through Instagram and live performances. Filmmakers can utilize various platforms like YouTube for trailers, TikTok for viral marketing, and film festivals for premiering their work. Understanding where your audience consumes content allows you to strategically position your offerings for maximum impact.

Promotion, the final P, relates to the tactics used to communicate the value of your product to your audience. This is where creativity and strategy intersect, particularly in the entertainment industry. Effective promotional strategies can include social media campaigns, influencer partnerships, email marketing, and public relations efforts. Utilizing celebrity endorsements can also amplify your brand's reach. For instance, a musician might collaborate with a popular influencer to showcase their new single, while a filmmaker could leverage a well-known actor to draw attention to their project. Engaging storytelling and visually compelling content are essential for capturing attention in a crowded marketplace.

In conclusion, mastering the Four Ps of Marketing— Product, Price, Place, and Promotion—is essential for anyone navigating the entertainment industry. By understanding each element and how they interrelate, musicians, filmmakers, influencers, and content creators can effectively build their brands and engage their audiences. This strategic approach not only enhances visibility but also fosters a deeper connection with fans, driving long-term success in an ever-evolving landscape.

Setting Clear Marketing Goals

Setting clear marketing goals is a crucial step for musicians, artists, filmmakers, influencers, and content creators aiming to carve their niche in the entertainment industry. Without defined objectives, efforts can easily become disorganized and ineffective, wasting both time and resources. Marketing goals provide a roadmap, allowing creators to strategically align their activities with their overarching vision. By establishing clear and measurable goals, individuals can track their progress, adapt their strategies as needed, and ultimately enhance their visibility and impact within the industry.

To effectively set marketing goals, it is essential to adhere to the SMART criteria: Specific, Measurable, Achievable, Relevant, and Time-bound. Specific goals eliminate ambiguity and provide direction. Rather than saying, "I want more followers," a more specific goal might be, "I want to gain 1,000 followers on Instagram within the next three months." Measurable goals allow for tracking progress; this could involve metrics such as social media engagement rates, ticket sales for an event, or streaming numbers. Achievable goals should stretch one's capabilities while remaining attainable; for instance, aiming for a 50% increase in streaming numbers may be unrealistic if the current metrics are low. Relevant goals align with broader career aspirations, ensuring that each objective contributes to long-term success. Finally, time- bound goals create urgency and motivate action, pushing creators to meet their targets within a set timeframe.

When setting these goals, it is also important to consider the unique characteristics of the entertainment industry. For example, musicians may focus on audience engagement tactics for streaming platforms, while filmmakers might prioritize event marketing for movie premieres and festivals. Influencers and content creators should aim for specific outcomes from partnerships and endorsements, such as increasing brand awareness or driving sales for a product.

Tailoring goals to fit individual niches not only enhances relevance but also allows for more effective strategy development.

Another key aspect of setting marketing goals is the necessity for flexibility. The entertainment landscape is constantly evolving, influenced by trends, audience preferences, and technological advancements. As a result, it is vital to regularly review and adjust marketing goals to reflect new insights and changes in the industry. Conducting periodic evaluations helps identify what strategies are working and which may need refinement. This adaptability ensures that creatives remain responsive to their audience and market dynamics, ultimately leading to more successful outcomes.

Lastly, collaboration and feedback play significant roles in the goal-setting process. Engaging with mentors, peers, or even fans can provide valuable perspectives that might highlight blind spots or inspire fresh ideas. Sharing marketing goals within a community can also foster accountability, encouraging individuals to stay committed to their objectives. By creating a supportive network, musicians, artists, filmmakers, influencers, and content creators can navigate the complexities of the entertainment industry more effectively, transforming their clear marketing goals into tangible achievements.

Chapter Four

Navigating Publicity Without a Publicist

Building Relationships with the Media

Building relationships with the media is a crucial aspect of navigating the entertainment industry, especially for musicians, artists, filmmakers, influencers, and content creators. A strong rapport with journalists, bloggers, and media outlets can significantly amplify your visibility and credibility. Unlike traditional public relations, which often relies on third-party professionals, DIY fame emphasizes the importance of directly engaging with the media to cultivate authentic relationships. This subchapter will outline key strategies for establishing and nurturing these connections, ultimately enhancing your brand and increasing your opportunities for exposure.

First and foremost, understanding the media landscape is essential. Familiarize yourself with the various types of media outlets and their audiences, including online publications, podcasts, radio shows, and television programs. Each platform has its unique focus and style, so tailor your approach accordingly. For instance, if you're an indie filmmaker, seek out film critics and bloggers who specialize in independent cinema. If you're a musician, engage with music journalists who cover your genre. Creating a targeted list of media contacts allows you to craft personalized pitches that resonate with their interests and audience, making it more likely that they will feature your work.

Once you've identified relevant media contacts, the next step is to reach out thoughtfully. A well-crafted pitch is your opportunity to make a strong first impression. Start with a compelling subject line that captures attention, followed by a concise and engaging introduction that highlights who you are and what you're promoting. Be sure to include any relevant achievements, unique angles, or timely aspects of your project that would interest the outlet. Follow up respectfully if you don't receive a response, but avoid being overly persistent. Building relationships takes time, and patience is key.

Engagement doesn't end with sending pitches. Actively follow and interact with the media professionals you're interested in connecting with. Share their articles on social media, comment on their posts, and engage in conversations that showcase your genuine interest in their work. This not only helps you stay on their radar but also demonstrates that you value their contributions to the industry. When they see you as a supportive figure rather than just a source for content, they are more likely to remember you and consider you for future stories or collaborations.

Lastly, once you've established a relationship and received coverage, it's vital to maintain that connection. Show appreciation for their support by thanking them publicly and privately. Share the coverage across your social media platforms, tagging the media outlet and the journalist. This not only showcases your gratitude but also brings additional visibility to their work. As you continue to produce new content, keep these media contacts updated with your latest projects and achievements. By nurturing these relationships over time, you create a network of allies in the industry who can help amplify your voice and brand, paving the way for future opportunities in your career.

Writing Press Releases That Get Noticed

Writing effective press releases is a crucial skill for anyone in the entertainment industry seeking to gain visibility and credibility. A well-crafted press release can serve as a powerful tool to announce a new album, a film premiere, or a significant collaboration. It acts as a bridge between your project and the media, providing journalists with the essential information they need to create compelling stories.

To stand out in a crowded marketplace, your press release must not only be informative but also engaging and tailored to your target audience.

The first step in writing a press release that gets noticed is to start with a strong headline. Your headline should be concise, catchy, and informative, capturing the essence of your announcement while piquing the interest of journalists and readers alike. Avoid jargon and focus on clarity; a clear headline will help ensure that your press release is picked up by media outlets. Following the headline, the subheadline can further elaborate on the key points, providing additional context that encourages readers to continue engaging with your content.

Next, begin the body of your press release with a compelling lead paragraph. This should answer the who, what, where, when, and why of your announcement. Use active voice and strong verbs to convey your message effectively. Consider the newsworthiness of your announcement—what makes it unique or timely? This is your chance to hook the reader, making them want to learn more. Be sure to include quotes from key individuals involved in the project, such as the artist, filmmaker, or influencer, as these can add a personal touch and lend credibility to your release.

As you develop the body of the press release, ensure that you provide relevant details that support your announcement. This could include background information about the project, key milestones, and any partnerships or endorsements that may amplify its significance. Use succinct paragraphs and bullet points to break up dense information, making it easier for journalists to skim and grasp the essential points quickly. Remember to keep your audience in mind; tailor your language and content to resonate with the specific niche you are targeting, whether it's music, film, or social media.

Finally, end your press release with a boilerplate—a brief paragraph that provides background on you or your organization. This section should summarize your mission, past achievements, and any relevant links to your website or social media profiles. A well- crafted boilerplate not only enhances your credibility but also encourages journalists to explore more about you and your work. Additionally, make sure to include contact information so that interested parties can easily follow up for more details. By adhering to these guidelines, you can create press releases that effectively capture attention and generate buzz in the entertainment industry.

Utilizing Online Platforms for Self- Promotion

In the contemporary landscape of the entertainment industry, self-promotion has become an indispensable skill for musicians, filmmakers, artists, and content creators. Online platforms serve as powerful tools that can amplify your reach, enhance your brand, and ultimately lead to greater opportunities in your career. By strategically utilizing these platforms, you can create a strong online presence that resonates with your target audience, fosters engagement, and converts followers into loyal fans or customers. Understanding how to navigate these digital spaces effectively is crucial for anyone looking to make a mark in their respective fields.

Social media platforms like Instagram, TikTok, and Twitter offer unique opportunities for self-promotion. Each platform caters to different demographics and content types, allowing you to tailor your approach accordingly. For instance, TikTok thrives on short, engaging video content, making it ideal for musicians seeking to showcase their talent or promote new releases. Instagram, with its visual focus, is perfect for artists wanting to display their work and connect with followers through stories and posts. By leveraging the strengths of each platform, you can create a cohesive and dynamic online presence that captures the attention of your audience.

In addition to social media, platforms such as YouTube and Twitch provide avenues for deeper engagement. Musicians can share music videos, behind-the-scenes footage, or live performances, while filmmakers can release trailers, interviews, and documentaries about their projects. These platforms not only allow for direct interaction with fans but also enable you to build a community around your brand. Engaging with your audience through comments, live streams, and Q&A sessions can foster a sense of loyalty and investment in your work, making your followers feel like active participants in your journey.

Email marketing is another vital component of online self-promotion that often gets overlooked. Building a mailing list allows you to communicate directly with your audience without relying solely on social media algorithms. Regular newsletters can keep your fans informed about upcoming projects, exclusive content, and merchandise releases. This form of direct communication not only strengthens your relationship with your audience but also drives traffic to your website or social media pages, enhancing your overall visibility. Crafting compelling email content that reflects your brand's voice is essential for maintaining engagement and interest.

Finally, collaborating with other creators and influencers in your niche can exponentially increase your reach. By partnering with individuals who share your values and aesthetics, you can tap into their audiences and gain exposure to new potential fans or customers. Whether it's co-hosting an event, participating in joint social media campaigns, or creating collaborative content, these partnerships can elevate your brand and broaden your visibility within the entertainment industry. In a world where connections are key, utilizing online platforms for self-promotion not only enhances your individual brand but also opens doors to exciting opportunities and collaborations.

Chapter Five

Social Media Strategy for Film and TV Promotions

Choosing the Right Platforms

Choosing the right platforms is a pivotal step in establishing your presence in the entertainment industry. With an array of options available, from social media networks to streaming services and traditional media outlets, the selection process can feel overwhelming. This subchapter will guide you through the considerations necessary to identify the optimal platforms for your specific needs as a musician, artist, filmmaker, influencer, or content creator. By understanding your audience, your content, and the unique attributes of each platform, you can maximize your reach and impact.

First and foremost, it is essential to define your target audience. Understanding who your audience is will inform your platform choices significantly. Are they primarily on Instagram, TikTok, Facebook, or YouTube?

Each platform attracts different demographics, and your content will resonate more effectively if it aligns with the preferences of your intended viewers. For instance, if you're a musician targeting a younger audience, platforms like TikTok and Instagram may be more advantageous due to their visual and short-form content styles.

Conversely, filmmakers might find more success on platforms like YouTube or Vimeo, where longer content can be showcased and engaged with.

Next, consider the content you create and how it fits within the parameters of various platforms. Each platform has its own strengths and weaknesses; some are designed for quick, engaging snippets while others allow for in-depth storytelling. Musicians can leverage platforms like Spotify and SoundCloud for audio distribution, while artists might explore Pinterest or Instagram for visual storytelling.

Filmmakers can utilize platforms like YouTube for trailers and behind-the-scenes content, as well as IMDb for professional networking and promotion. By aligning your content with the right platform, you enhance the likelihood of engagement and visibility.

Another critical factor in choosing the right platforms is the nature of your branding and the message you want to convey. Consistency across platforms is vital for building a recognizable brand. If your work reflects a particular aesthetic or message, select platforms that will not only support but amplify that identity. For example, a filmmaker focusing on indie horror films may find that horror- centric communities on platforms like Reddit or niche film forums provide a more engaged audience than broader social media sites. In contrast, a musician with a vibrant, colorful persona may thrive on visually driven platforms where aesthetics play a key role.

25 Online Self-Promotion Tools for the Entertainment Industry and Why to Use Them

1. Instagram

Why Use It: Instagram is a highly visual platform, perfect for promoting content in the entertainment industry. With features like Stories, Reels, and IGTV, you can share short clips, behind-the-scenes moments, and polished performances, making it ideal for artists, actors, and musicians to build their brands.

2. Youtube

Why Use It: YouTube is the go-to platform for video content, with a global audience. Whether you're uploading music videos, comedy sketches, or short films, YouTube offers creators the chance to monetize their content through ads, grow their audience, and establish their brand.

3. TikTok

Why Use It: TikTok's algorithm-driven content discovery makes it one of the fastest ways to go viral. The platform's emphasis on short-form video content is perfect for showcasing creativity, trends, and performances, helping artists, musicians, and creators gain followers quickly.

4. **Spotify for Artists**

   Why Use It: Musicians can use Spotify for Artists to track their streams, analyze listener demographics, and promote their music on one of the largest streaming platforms. Spotify's playlist feature also offers opportunities for massive exposure.

5. **X Formerly Known as Twitter**

   Why Use It: Twitter is a great tool for real-time communication, engagement with fans, and networking within the entertainment industry. It allows artists to participate in trending conversations and share quick updates or promotional content.

6. **Patreon**

   Why Use It: Patreon provides a platform for creators to monetize their content by offering exclusive perks to paying subscribers. It's perfect for musicians, writers, and artists looking to build a steady income stream directly from their fanbase.

7. **SoundCloud**

   Why Use It: SoundCloud is a community-driven platform for musicians to share their tracks, engage with listeners, and network with other artists. It's a great place for independent musicians to get feedback and build a following.

8. **LinkedIn**

   Why Use It: LinkedIn is valuable for networking within the entertainment industry, connecting with industry professionals, and showcasing your achievements in a more formal setting. It's ideal for building a professional reputation and securing business opportunities.

9. **Twitch**

   Why Use It: Twitch is a live streaming platform that allows performers, musicians, and artists to interact with fans in real-time. Its monetization options, such as subscriptions and donations, make it a great tool for building a loyal fanbase.

10. Facebook

Why Use It: Facebook remains a powerful tool for connecting with a broad audience. Its event and group features are particularly useful for promoting live shows, tours, or fan communities, while its advertising tools allow for targeted promotions.

11. Bandcamp

Why Use It: Bandcamp allows musicians to sell their music and merchandise directly to fans. It's a platform that offers more control over pricing and revenue, making it ideal for independent artists.

12. Pinterest

Why Use It: Pinterest is a visual discovery platform that can help artists and creators drive traffic to their content. Whether promoting visual artwork, music videos, or fashion, Pinterest's image- based search can increase visibility and engagement.

13. Clubhouse

Why Use It: Clubhouse is an audio-based social networking app where users can join and participate in live discussions. It's an excellent platform for networking, hosting industry discussions, and connecting with other creatives in real-time.

14. Reddit

Why Use It: Reddit is a community-driven platform where creators can share their work and engage with niche audiences. Subreddits tailored to specific entertainment industries can be powerful tools for networking and gaining feedback.

15. Medium

Why Use It: Medium is a publishing platform that allows writers, filmmakers, and creators to share their thoughts and stories. It's ideal for building thought leadership, sharing behind-the- scenes insights, or promoting new projects through written content.

16. Vimeo

Why Use It: Vimeo is a video-sharing platform known for its high-quality content and professional community. It's ideal for filmmakers, animators, and videographers who want to showcase their work in a polished and artistic environment.

17. Snapchat

Why Use It: Snapchat's ephemeral content is great for sharing spontaneous, behind-the-scenes moments with your audience. It's especially popular with younger demographics and offers opportunities for real-time engagement.

18. Ko-fi

Why Use It: Ko-fi is a platform that allows creators to receive small donations or "tips" from their fans. It's a simple and easy way to monetize your content without the commitment of a subscription model.

19. Anchor

Why Use It: Anchor is a podcast creation and distribution platform that simplifies the process of getting your audio content onto platforms like Spotify and Apple Podcasts. It's ideal for creators looking to expand their brand into podcasting.

20. Dribbble

Why Use It: Dribbble is a platform for visual artists, designers, and illustrators to showcase their portfolios. It's an excellent tool for creatives in the visual arts to gain exposure and connect with potential clients or collaborators.

21. Substack

Why Use It: Substack allows creators to monetize newsletters by offering subscription-based content. Writers, filmmakers, and industry commentators can use this platform to build a dedicated audience around their ideas and insights.

22. **Mixcloud**

Why Use It: Mixcloud is a platform for DJs and radio hosts to share mixes, podcasts, and radio shows. It's ideal for those in the music industry looking to grow their audience and gain exposure through audio content.

23. **Behance**

Why Use It: Behance is an online portfolio platform for creative professionals in fields like photography, graphic design, and illustration. It's a great place to showcase your work and network with other professionals.

24. **ReverbNation**

Why Use It: ReverbNation is a platform designed specifically for musicians, offering tools for distribution, promotion, and fan engagement. It's a one-stop-shop for independent artists looking to grow their careers.

25. **Discord**

Why Use It: Discord is a communication platform that allows creators to build and manage their own communities. It's a versatile tool for creating fan groups, hosting discussions, and engaging directly with your audience in a more personal setting.

Conclusion

These 25 online tools provide a range of options for creators in the entertainment industry to promote their work, build an audience, and establish their brand.

Whether through visual content, music, live streaming, or networking, each platform offers unique opportunities for self-promotion, enabling artists and entertainers to take control of their careers and reach their goals. By strategically utilizing these tools, you can grow your presence, connect with fans, and thrive in the competitive world of entertainment.

Lastly, it's important to stay adaptable and open to exploring new platforms as they emerge. The digital landscape is continually evolving, and what works today may not necessarily work tomorrow. Regularly assess your engagement metrics and audience feedback to ensure your platform choices remain effective. Experimenting with new platforms and tools can open up fresh avenues for audience engagement and content distribution. By remaining flexible and informed about industry trends, you can effectively navigate the ever-changing dynamics of the entertainment industry and maintain a strong connection with your audience.

Content Creation Tips for Engagement

Content creation is a pivotal aspect of building engagement in the entertainment industry. Musicians, artists, filmmakers, influencers, and content creators must harness effective strategies to capture their audience's attention and foster lasting connections. In an environment saturated with content, understanding the nuances of your audience and delivering compelling material is key. This subchapter outlines essential tips for creating engaging content that not only entertains but also cultivates a loyal following.

First and foremost, authenticity is crucial in your content creation endeavors. Audiences can easily discern when content feels forced or insincere. By sharing your genuine self—your struggles, triumphs, and unique perspectives— you establish an emotional connection that resonates with viewers. This authenticity extends beyond personal narratives; it also encompasses the values and messages you choose to promote. Aligning your content with your core beliefs fosters trust and encourages viewers to engage with your work on a deeper level.

Visual storytelling holds immense power in capturing audience attention, especially in the entertainment industry where aesthetics play a significant role. High-quality visuals, whether through photography, videography, or graphic design, can significantly enhance your content's appeal. Invest time in learning basic design principles and utilizing tools that allow you to create striking visuals that reflect your brand. Consistency in visual style across platforms reinforces your identity and makes your content more recognizable, encouraging repeat engagement.

Moreover, interactivity is a vital component of modern content creation. Engaging your audience through polls, Q&A sessions, or live streams invites participation and creates a two-way conversation. This interactive approach not only enriches the viewer experience but also provides valuable insights into audience preferences and interests. By actively involving your audience, you transform passive viewers into active participants, thereby fostering a sense of community around your brand.

Finally, leveraging data analytics to refine your content strategy can significantly enhance engagement. Use metrics from social media platforms, website traffic, and audience interactions to understand what resonates with your audience. Analyzing trends and preferences allows you to tailor your content to meet their expectations, increasing the likelihood of engagement. Regularly revisiting and adjusting your strategy based on these insights helps ensure that your content remains relevant and captivating in an ever-evolving digital landscape.

In conclusion, effective content creation for engagement in the entertainment industry hinges on authenticity, visual appeal, interactivity, and data- informed strategies. By embracing these principles, musicians, artists, filmmakers, influencers, and content creators can craft compelling narratives and experiences that not only capture attention but also cultivate a dedicated audience. In a world where content is abundant, the ability to engage meaningfully sets you apart and paves the way for enduring success.

Analyzing Metrics and Adjusting Strategies

In the rapidly evolving landscape of the entertainment industry, understanding and analyzing metrics is crucial for musicians, artists, filmmakers, influencers, and content creators. Metrics provide valuable insights into audience behavior, engagement levels, and overall effectiveness of marketing strategies. By closely monitoring key performance indicators (KPIs) such as social media engagement rates, streaming numbers, and website traffic, creatives can identify trends and patterns that inform their promotional efforts. This analytical approach empowers individuals to make data-driven decisions, ultimately enhancing their ability to reach and engage their target audience.One of the first steps in analyzing metrics is establishing clear objectives. Whether the goal is to increase album sales, grow a social media following, or boost attendance at a film premiere, defining specific, measurable objectives is essential. Once these goals are set, measuring progress through relevant metrics becomes straightforward. For example, a musician aiming to increase concert attendance can track ticket sales over time, correlating spikes with social media campaigns or influencer endorsements. This connection highlights which strategies are effective and which may require reevaluation.

Adjusting strategies based on metric analysis is equally important. The entertainment industry is dynamic, and what works today may not resonate tomorrow. For instance, if social media engagement for a film's promotional campaign begins to decline, it may be time to pivot toward a different platform or adopt a fresh content approach. Engaging with audience feedback, whether through comments, reviews, or direct messages, can also provide invaluable insights. By actively listening and adapting to audience preferences, creators can foster a loyal fan base that feels invested in their work.

Collaboration with analytics tools can further enhance the ability to track and interpret metrics. Platforms such as Google Analytics, social media insights, and specialized marketing software offer detailed reports that break down audience demographics, behaviors, and engagement rates. These insights can reveal not only how many people are interacting with content but also the quality of that engagement. For example, understanding which posts drive the most shares or comments can help refine future content strategies. Integrating these tools into regular marketing practices can create a more responsive and effective promotional strategy.

Ultimately, the process of analyzing metrics and adjusting strategies is an ongoing cycle. As the entertainment landscape shifts, so too must the tactics employed by musicians, filmmakers, and influencers. Continuous learning and adaptation are key to sustaining relevance and success in this competitive industry. By embracing a data-driven mindset, creators can enhance their visibility, strengthen their brand, and better connect with their audience, ensuring that they remain at the forefront of the entertainment scene.

Chapter Six

Event Marketing for Movie Premieres and Festivals

Planning and Executing Successful Events

Planning and executing successful events is a crucial aspect of building your brand and gaining visibility in the entertainment industry. For musicians, artists, filmmakers, influencers, and content creators, events provide an opportunity to showcase talent, forge connections, and engage with audiences in meaningful ways. A well-organized event not only amplifies your public presence but can also serve as a powerful marketing tool, helping to establish partnerships, attract endorsements, and create buzz around your projects. This subchapter will outline key strategies for effectively planning and executing events that resonate with your target audience.

The first step in event planning is to define your objectives clearly. Are you looking to promote a new album, film, or content piece? Are you aiming to engage with fans or attract industry professionals? By identifying your goals, you can tailor your event to meet specific outcomes, whether that's increasing ticket sales, boosting social media engagement, or securing sponsorships.

Additionally, understanding your target audience is essential. Consider their preferences, demographics, and interests to ensure the event aligns with what they value. This foundational work sets the stage for a successful event that speaks directly to your intended audience.

Once your objectives are established, the next phase involves logistics. Selecting the right venue is vital; it should not only accommodate your audience but also reflect your brand's identity. Whether it's an intimate acoustic show at a local café or a large-scale premiere at a historic theater, the venue should resonate with the theme of your event. Don't forget to factor in the date and time – avoid scheduling against major industry events to maximize attendance. Additionally, create a detailed timeline to keep your preparations on track, covering everything from booking talent and vendors to marketing the event and managing ticket sales.

Marketing your event is equally important and requires a multifaceted approach. Utilize social media platforms to create buzz, share behind-the-scenes content, and engage directly with your fans.

Collaborate with other creators or influencers to reach broader audiences and leverage their networks. Email marketing remains a powerful tool; sending out newsletters to your existing fan base can help keep them informed and excited. Furthermore, consider integrating brand partnerships and sponsorships to enhance the event experience and provide additional promotional opportunities. This strategy not only adds credibility but can also alleviate some financial burdens associated with hosting events.

Finally, executing the event successfully is all about attention to detail and adaptability. Ensure a smooth check-in process, provide clear signage, and have a dedicated team to address any issues that may arise. Engaging with attendees during the event can foster a sense of community; consider interactive elements like Q&A sessions, meet-and-greets, or live social media interactions. After the event, follow up with attendees through thank-you emails and share highlights across your platforms to maintain engagement. Collecting feedback can also provide valuable insights for future events, allowing you to refine your approach and continue building your presence in the entertainment industry.

Collaborating with Influencers and Partners

Collaborating with influencers and partners is an essential strategy for musicians, artists, filmmakers, and content creators seeking to build their brand and expand their reach within the entertainment industry. In today's digital landscape, influencers possess the ability to sway public opinion and drive engagement, making them valuable allies for promoting projects, products, and events. By aligning with the right influencers, creators can tap into established audiences and leverage their credibility to enhance visibility. Understanding how to cultivate these relationships is crucial for anyone looking to navigate the complexities of modern publicity and marketing.

The first step in successful collaboration is identifying influencers who resonate with your brand and target audience. This involves researching potential partners whose values, aesthetics, and content align with your own. For musicians, this could mean connecting with influencers who focus on music reviews, lifestyle content, or even fashion. Filmmakers might consider partnering with film critics, cinema bloggers, or popular YouTubers who specialize in movie analysis.

The key is to ensure that the influencers you choose not only have an engaged following but also share a genuine interest in your work, as authenticity can significantly amplify the impact of your promotional efforts.

Once potential collaborators are identified, the next step is to reach out with a clear proposal that outlines mutual benefits. Successful partnerships thrive on a foundation of reciprocity; therefore, it's essential to articulate what you can offer influencers in return for their support. This could range from exclusive content, behind-the-scenes access, or merchandise, to financial compensation or promotional support on your own channels.

Highlighting the value of collaboration for both parties fosters a sense of partnership and encourages influencers to invest their time and energy into promoting your projects.

Effective collaboration also extends beyond one-off promotions. Building long-term relationships with influencers can yield ongoing benefits and create a network of support. Regular engagement and communication can help solidify these partnerships, ensuring that influencers remain excited and invested in your brand. Consider creating a community around your work, where influencers feel like they are part of a larger narrative. This could involve inviting them to events, providing updates on projects, or even collaborating on creative endeavors, such as music videos or film trailers that showcase both your art and their influence.

Finally, measuring the success of your collaborations is vital for understanding their impact and refining your strategies. Utilize analytics tools to track engagement metrics, audience reach, and conversion rates from influencer campaigns. By analyzing this data, you can gain insights into what types of collaborations resonate most with your audience and adjust your approach accordingly. Regularly assessing the effectiveness of your partnerships will not only enhance your future collaborations but also help you build a robust marketing strategy that aligns with your goals in the entertainment industry.

Maximizing Media Coverage for Your Events

Maximizing media coverage for your events is essential for building visibility and generating buzz, especially in the competitive landscape of the entertainment industry. Whether you are a musician launching a new album, a filmmaker premiering a project, or an influencer hosting a live event, strategic media engagement can elevate your profile and draw in a larger audience. This subchapter will explore effective tactics to ensure that your events receive the attention they deserve, leveraging both traditional media outlets and the power of social media.

First, it's crucial to prepare a compelling press kit that includes relevant information about your event, such as the date, location, purpose, and any notable guests or performances.

This kit should also feature high-quality images and videos that capture the essence of your brand and the excitement of your event. Distributing this press kit to local media, entertainment blogs, and industry influencers can significantly enhance your outreach efforts. Personalizing your communication to each recipient can also increase the likelihood of coverage, as tailored pitches show that you have done your research and understand their audience.

Utilizing social media effectively is another key component of maximizing media coverage. Create a dedicated event hashtag to encourage attendees and fans to share their experiences. This not only builds excitement but also allows you to track conversations and engagement surrounding your event. Engaging with your followers through behind-the-scenes content, countdowns, and interactive posts can create a sense of community and anticipation. Additionally, consider collaborating with influencers who align with your brand to amplify your reach; their endorsement can validate your event and attract their followers, potentially expanding your audience significantly.

In addition to digital strategies, hosting media-friendly activities during your event can draw the attention of journalists and bloggers. Consider organizing a press conference, a VIP lounge, or exclusive interviews with key attendees. Providing unique photo opportunities or interactive experiences can make your event more appealing to the media. Remember, journalists are always on the lookout for fresh stories, and by creating engaging narratives around your event, you increase your chances of receiving extensive coverage that goes beyond standard announcements.

25 Tips and Tools for Event Marketing for Movie Premieres and Festivals

1. **Create a Compelling Event Website**

   Why Use It: A dedicated website for your movie premiere or festival acts as a central hub for all event-related information. Include details like event schedules, ticketing information, trailers, and updates.

   Platforms like Wix or Squarespace allow for easy creation of visually appealing sites that align with your event's branding.

2. **Leverage Social Media Campaigns**

   Why Use It: Use platforms like Instagram, Facebook, Twitter, and TikTok to promote your event. Create teasers, behind-the-scenes content, and countdowns leading up to the premiere or festival. Hashtag campaigns can also increase visibility and encourage user-generated content.

3. **Utilize Eventbrite for Ticketing**

   Why Use It: Eventbrite is a popular ticketing platform that allows you to sell tickets, manage attendees, and promote your event. Its built-in promotional tools can help you reach potential attendees through email campaigns and social media ads.

4. Collaborate with Influencers

Why Use It: Partnering with social media influencers or film critics who align with your movie or festival's target audience can boost visibility. Influencers can promote the event to their followers, creating buzz and driving ticket sales.

5. Use Facebook Events

Why Use It: Facebook Events is a powerful tool for event marketing. It allows you to create an event page, invite people, and track RSVPs. You can also promote the event through paid ads to reach a broader audience, especially within local or niche communities.

6. Email Marketing Campaigns

Why Use It: Tools like Mailchimp or Constant Contact allow you to build email lists and send targeted email campaigns. Regular updates, special offers, and exclusive content through emails keep potential attendees engaged and informed about your event.

7. Press Releases and Media Outreach

Why Use It: Traditional media coverage is still essential for event marketing. Craft a compelling press release and distribute it to relevant media outlets, film blogs, and industry publications. Tools like PR Newswire or Cision can help distribute your press release to a wide audience.

8. Teaser Trailers and Video Ads

Why Use It: Creating short teaser trailers or video ads is a great way to generate excitement.

These can be shared on social media, YouTube, or embedded in your event website. Platforms like Vimeo or YouTube Ads allow for targeted video promotion to reach relevant audiences.

9. Leverage Google Ads

Why Use It: Google Ads allows you to target specific demographics with your event promotion. Create ads that drive traffic to your event website, sell tickets, or promote special offers. Google Ads offers robust targeting options, ensuring you reach the right audience.

10. **Collaborate with Local Businesses**

Why Use It: Partnering with local businesses can increase event visibility. Local cafes, bookstores, and theaters might be willing to promote your event in exchange for cross-promotion. You can offer them branded promotional materials like posters and flyers to display in their establishments.

11. **Event Hashtags**

Why Use It: Create a unique hashtag for your movie premiere or festival and encourage attendees to use it in their social media posts. This not only increases online visibility but also helps aggregate user- generated content, making it easier to track conversations about your event.

12. **Sponsor Collaborations**

Why Use It: Partnering with relevant brands or sponsors can help fund your event while providing additional promotional channels. Sponsors often promote events they are involved in, expanding your event's reach to their audiences.

Platforms like SponsorMyEvent can help connect you with potential sponsors.

13. **Photo Booths and Red Carpet Experiences**

Why Use It: Setting up photo booths or red carpet experiences at your event encourages attendees to share their experience online. Branded backdrops and photo props can help promote your movie premiere or festival on social media.

14. **Utilize Event Marketing Software**

Why Use It: Tools like Bizzabo, Splash, or Cvent streamline event marketing by managing everything from ticket sales to attendee

engagement. These platforms often include promotional features like email marketing, social media integration, and data
analytics to optimize your event's reach.

15. **Paid Social Media Advertising**
Why Use It: Platforms like Facebook, Instagram, and LinkedIn
allow you to create targeted ads to promote your event to specific
demographics. Paid social ads can significantly boost your event's
visibility and drive more ticket sales or RSVPs.

16. **Create a Blog or Content Series**
Why Use It: Blogging or creating a content series around your
event can build anticipation. Share interviews with filmmakers,
behind-the-scenes content, or insights into the festival program-
ming. Content marketing platforms like Medium or your event's
website blog can help reach an engaged audience.

17. **Influencer Takeovers**
Why Use It: Allow influencers or filmmakers to take over your social media accounts for a day. This gives your followers a unique
perspective on your event while also leveraging the influencer's
fanbase to promote your movie premiere or festival.

18. **Use a Countdown Timer**
Why Use It: Adding a countdown timer to your event website
or social media pages creates a sense of urgency. Tools like
Countdown Timer for WordPress or TickCounter can be embedded easily into your digital platforms to build excitement as the
event date approaches.

19. **Offer Early Bird Discounts**
Why Use It: Early bird pricing encourages attendees to buy tickets sooner, creating buzz and ensuring a solid turnout. Using
platforms like Eventbrite or Brown Paper Tickets, you can set
up tiered pricing and promote limited-time offers through your
marketing channels.

20. **Create a VIP Experience**

Why Use It: Offering a VIP experience with exclusive perks like meet-and-greets, reserved seating, or branded swag can create a premium appeal to your event. Promote VIP packages through your website, social media, and email campaigns to attract high-value attendees.

21. **Geofencing and Location-Based Marketing**

Why Use It: Geofencing allows you to target ads to users within a specific geographic area. This is particularly useful for local movie premieres and festivals, as it enables you to promote your event to people near the venue. Platforms like Blis and GroundTruth offer geofencing solutions.

22. **Create Event Apps**

Why Use It: Custom event apps offer attendees a personalized experience. With apps like Whova or EventMobi, you can provide schedules, maps, and real-time updates directly to your attendees' phones, enhancing their experience and engagement at your event.

23. **Partner with Film Schools or Industry Groups**

Why Use It: Collaborating with film schools or industry organizations can help you tap into a network of film enthusiasts, students, and professionals. These partnerships can provide you with promotional support and access to a built-in audience that is already interested in your event's content.

24. **Run a Contest or Giveaway**

Why Use It: Running a contest or giveaway for tickets, swag, or VIP passes generates excitement and increases social media engagement. Use tools like Rafflecopter or Gleam to run the contest and require participants to share your event or follow your social media accounts to enter.

25. **Live Stream the Event**

Why Use It: Live streaming parts of your event (like the red carpet, Q&As, or performances) can extend your event's reach beyond the physical attendees. Platforms like YouTube Live, Instagram Live, or Facebook Live allow you to engage with a global audience, creating a broader impact and potentially increasing future attendance.

Conclusion

These 25 tools and tips offer a comprehensive approach to marketing movie premieres and festivals in the digital age. By combining traditional media outreach with modern digital strategies, you can create a multi-faceted event marketing campaign that builds buzz, drives ticket sales, and ensures a successful event.

Lastly, follow up after your event with a recap that includes highlights, media coverage links, and testimonials from attendees. Sharing this information through your social media channels and mailing lists can keep the momentum going and attract future interest. Documenting your event through video highlights or photo galleries can also serve as valuable content, providing material for future marketing efforts. By implementing these strategies, you can maximize media coverage for your events, ultimately enhancing your visibility and establishing a stronger presence in the entertainment industry.

Chapter Seven

Celebrity Endorsements and Partnerships

Identifying the Right Celebrities for Your Brand

Identifying the right celebrities for your brand is a crucial step in establishing a successful partnership that can elevate your visibility and credibility within the entertainment industry. The first step in this process is understanding your brand's identity and objectives. Are you looking to enhance your image, reach a specific audience, or increase sales? Once you have clarity on your goals, you can begin searching for celebrities whose public persona and values align with your brand. A mismatch can lead to ineffective campaigns or even backlash, so a thorough alignment analysis is essential.

Consider the target demographics of both your brand and potential celebrity partners. Each celebrity has a unique fan base, which can vary widely in age, interests, and purchasing behavior. Use analytics tools to gather data on the demographics of a celebrity's followers and analyze how they match with your target audience. For example, if you're a musician aiming to promote an upcoming album, partnering with a celebrity who resonates with your music genre and has a fan base that mirrors your target listeners will amplify your reach and engagement.

Another vital aspect to consider is the celebrity's recent activities and public image. It's not just about their star power; their current relevance and the sentiment surrounding them play a significant role in how effective a partnership may be. A celebrity embroiled in controversy may not be the best choice, even if they have a large following. Research recent interviews, social media posts, and public appearances to gauge their current standing. An ideal partner should have a positive reputation and be actively engaging with their audience, as this can enhance your brand's reputation by association.

Authenticity is also key when selecting a celebrity for endorsement. Today's audiences are savvy and can often sense when a partnership feels forced or insincere. Look for celebrities who have a genuine affinity for your product or message. This could be an artist who has publicly supported similar causes or a filmmaker who shares a passion for independent cinema. Genuine endorsements resonate more with audiences and can lead to higher engagement rates and conversion.

Finally, consider the potential for long-term collaboration rather than a one-off promotion. Building a relationship with a celebrity can provide ongoing benefits and create a narrative that resonates with audiences over time. This approach allows for deeper storytelling and can integrate your brand into the celebrity's larger narrative, enhancing visibility across multiple platforms. As you navigate this process, keep in mind that the right celebrity partnership can serve as a powerful catalyst for your brand, driving engagement and fostering a lasting connection with your audience.

25 Tips on How to Get Celebrity Endorsements and Partnerships and Where to Go to Get Them (with Resources)

1. **Define Your Brand's Unique Value Proposition (UVP)**
   Why: Celebrities align with brands that reflect their image. Ensure your brand stands out by clearly defining what makes it unique. Highlight how it can add value to the celebrity's public persona.

   Where to Go: Work with branding consultants or agencies like Brand Consultancy, which can help refine your UVP.

2. **Target Celebrities Who Align with Your Brand**
   Why: Focus on celebrities whose personal brand, values, and audience align with your product or service.

   Authentic partnerships are more likely to succeed.

   Where to Go: Use tools like IMDBPro to research celebrities' interests, upcoming projects, and representation.

3. **Work with Talent Agencies**
   Why: Talent agencies represent celebrities and can connect you with the right individuals for endorsements. They help negotiate deals and manage the process.

   Where to Go: Agencies like Creative Artists Agency (CAA), United Talent Agency (UTA) and William Morris Endeavor (WME) specialize in celebrity partnerships.

4. **Use Celebrity Endorsement Platforms**
   Why: Platforms specifically designed for connecting brands with celebrities streamline the process.

   These platforms offer vetted connections and ease communication.

   Where to Go: Check out Celebrity Edorsers, Influence.co and Captiv8 for direct access to celebrities and influencers.

5. **Leverage Social Media for Direct Outreach**
   Why: Many celebrities and their teams use social media for business inquiries. Direct messages can sometimes bypass traditional gatekeepers.

   Where to Go: Reach out through Instagram, Twitter or LinkedIN. Tools like SocialRank help identify and connect with key influencers.

6. **Attend Industry Events**
   Why: Industry events, film festivals, and award shows provide opportunities to network with celebrities and their teams in person, making introductions and building relationships.

   Where to Go: Events like Cannes Film Festival, Sundance Film Festival and The Oscars are prime for networking. Use Eventbrite to find industry-specific events.

7. **Hire a PR Firm**
Why: Public relations firms specializing in celebrity endorsements can facilitate partnerships by using their industry connections and expertise.

Where to Go: Firms like Publicity Brand PR, 42West and Rogers & Cowan PMK specialize in entertainment PR and celebrity endorsements.

8. **Create Compelling Campaigns**
Why: Celebrities are drawn to campaigns that allow them to creatively engage. Offer them the chance to co-create content that enhances their personal brand.

Where to Go: Use creative agencies like Publicity Brand PR or TBWA\Chiat\Day to help design campaigns that attract celebrity interest.

9. **Offer Equity or Ownership Stakes**
Why: Many celebrities prefer to have a stake in the companies they endorse. Offering equity can incentivize deeper, long-term involvement.

Where to Go: Consider consulting with Venture Capital Firms like Andreessen Horowitz or First Round Capital that have experience structuring equity deals in partnerships.

10. **Collaborate with Charities or Causes They Support**
Why: Celebrities are often passionate about philanthropy. Aligning your brand with their charitable causes can create a meaningful partnership.

Where to Go: Use platforms like Charity Navigator to identify charities that celebrities support and explore collaboration opportunities.

11. **Engage Influencers as a Starting Point**

Why: Influencers can serve as a stepping stone to securing larger celebrity endorsements. Their audiences are often engaged, and successful partnerships can lead to bigger opportunities.

Where to Go: Platforms like Influencity, BuzzSumo and AspireIQ can help you find relevant influencers.

12. **Participate in Sponsorship Opportunities**

Why: Sponsoring events that celebrities attend or participate in can increase your brand's visibility and create networking opportunities.

Where to Go: Use sponsorship platforms like SponsorMyEvent or SponsorPitch to find events and festivals that attract celebrity attendees.

13. **Offer Exclusive Product Collaborations**

Why: Celebrities are more likely to endorse a product that feels exclusive. Consider creating a limited edition product or collaboration that they can co-brand.

Where to Go: Collaborate with design agencies like IDEO or Pentagram to create bespoke products that appeal to celebrity tastes.

14. **Use Celebrity Management Companies**

Why: Celebrity management companies oversee a celebrity's career and can facilitate endorsement deals. Approaching them directly can lead to partnerships.

Where to Go: Companies like Publicity Brand PR, Full Picture, and ICM Partners specialize in celebrity management and endorsements.

15. **Host VIP Events**
Why: Hosting exclusive VIP events can attract celebrity atten-dees. These events offer networking opportunities in a more intimate setting.

Where to Go: Use event management platforms like Cvent or Bizzabo to plan and promote VIP experiences.

16. **Engage with Celebrity Assistants and Managers**
Why: Celebrity assistants and managers are often the first point of contact for endorsement inquiries. Building relationships with them can lead to successful partnerships.

Where to Go: Use professional networking platforms like Linkedin to connect with celebrity assistants and managers.

17. **Leverage Media and Press Coverage**
Why: Getting media attention for your brand can attract celebri-ty endorsements. Celebrities often want to be associated with brands that are trending and have a strong media presence.

Where to Go: Platforms like HARO (Help a Reporter Out) and Cision can help you secure media coverage and generate buzz.

18. **Use Entertainment Marketing Firms**
Why: Entertainment marketing firms specialize in connecting brands with celebrities for endorsements and collaborations. They can guide you through the process and secure top talent.

Where to Go: Agencies like Publicity Brand PR, BrandMark, and Celebrity Talent International focus on entertainment marketing.

19. **Utilize Celebrity Endorsement Databases**
Why: Databases that track celebrity endorsements and partner-ships can help you identify potential opportunities and trends.

Where to Go: Use tools like Celebrity Intelligence and Famous-Birthdays to research celebrity endorsement history and preferences.

20. **Offer Social Impact Partnerships**
Why: Celebrities often seek partnerships that offer social impact. Highlight how your brand contributes to positive change in the world, and it may attract a celebrity's attention.

Where to Go: Collaborate with platforms like Benevity or GlobalGiving to create impactful social campaigns that appeal to celebrities.

21. **Sponsor Celebrity Golf Tournaments or Fundraisers**
Why: Celebrity golf tournaments and charity fundraisers offer opportunities to meet and network with celebrities in a relaxed environment.

Where to Go: Websites like Charitybuzz or Charity Navigator list celebrity charity events and sponsorship opportunities.

22. **Participate in Entertainment Industry Panels and Conferences**
Why: Speaking at or attending industry panels and conferences can position your brand as an expert in its field, making it more attractive to celebrities looking for strategic partnerships.

Where to Go: Attend or sponsor panels at conferences like SXSW, Cannes Lions, and Variety's Entertainment Summit.

23. **Offer Personal Experiences or Perks**
Why: Celebrities appreciate unique, personalized experiences. Offering exclusive perks like VIP travel, private events, or custom products can make your brand more enticing.

Where to Go: Partner with luxury travel or event companies like Black Tomato or Quintessentially to offer high-end experiences.

24. **Highlight Mutual Benefits**

Why: Celebrities are more likely to endorse your brand if there are mutual benefits. Emphasize how the partnership can enhance their public image, align with their goals, or expand their influence.

Where to Go: Collaborate with strategic marketing consultants like Publicity Brand PR or McKinsey & Company to outline the mutual benefits in your pitch.

25. **Be Prepared for Long-Term Collaborations**

Why: Celebrities often look for long-term partnerships rather than one-off deals. Position your brand as a long-term collaborator, offering opportunities for sustained involvement.

Where to Go: Use platforms like Upfluence or CreatorIQ to manage influencer and celebrity relationships over time, ensuring the partnership evolves and remains mutually beneficial.

Conclusion

These 25 tips and resources provide a comprehensive guide to securing celebrity endorsements and partnerships. By leveraging the right platforms, agencies, and strategies, you can build successful relationships that elevate your brand and broaden its reach in the entertainment industry.

Negotiating Deals and Contracts

Negotiating deals and contracts is a critical skill for musicians, artists, filmmakers, influencers, and content creators navigating the entertainment industry.

Understanding the nuances of these negotiations can significantly impact your career trajectory, financial stability, and creative control. This subchapter will explore key strategies for effectively negotiating deals, ensuring that you secure the best terms while maintaining your artistic integrity.

The first step in successful negotiation is preparation. Before entering any discussions, it's vital to conduct thorough research on the parties involved, the industry standards for similar contracts, and the specific terms you wish to negotiate. Familiarize yourself with common clauses, such as payment structures, rights to content, and duration of agreements. Knowing what is typical in your niche can empower you to advocate for yourself effectively. Additionally, consider your long-term goals and how each deal aligns with your vision. This clarity will guide your negotiations and help you identify which terms are non-negotiable.

Building rapport with the other party is equally crucial in the negotiation process. Establishing a positive relationship can lead to more fruitful discussions and foster a collaborative atmosphere. Approach negotiations with a mindset of partnership rather than confrontation. Use active listening to understand the other party's needs and concerns, which can open pathways to mutually beneficial solutions. By demonstrating respect and professionalism, you not only increase your chances of a favorable outcome but also lay the groundwork for future collaborations.

When it comes to the actual negotiation, clarity and assertiveness are key. Clearly articulate your needs and expectations, and do not shy away from discussing your value in the context of the deal. Whether it's your unique audience, your creative vision, or your past successes, make sure the other party understands what you bring to the table. Be prepared to counter offers and provide justifications for your requests. Remember, negotiation is often a back-and-forth process, and flexibility can lead to innovative solutions that satisfy both parties.

Finally, always seek legal counsel when finalizing any contract. A professional can help you navigate complex legal language and identify any potential pitfalls that could affect your rights as a creator. Ensure that all agreements are documented in writing and that you fully understand the implications of each clause before signing. By arming yourself with knowledge, building relationships, and maintaining a professional demeanor, you can effectively negotiate deals and contracts that support your career in the ever-evolving entertainment industry.

Leveraging Endorsements for Maximum Impact

Leveraging endorsements effectively can be a game- changer for musicians, artists, filmmakers, and influencers aiming to carve out a distinct space in the entertainment industry. An endorsement can serve as a powerful tool, enhancing credibility and expanding reach when executed thoughtfully. This subchapter will explore strategic approaches to harnessing endorsements, focusing on the nuances of celebrity partnerships, social media influence, and event marketing to maximize impact.

To begin with, identifying the right endorsements is crucial. The alignment between your brand and the endorser's image must resonate authentically with your target audience. For musicians, this could mean collaborating with well-known artists in a similar genre or lifestyle influencers who embody your brand ethos.

Filmmakers might seek endorsements from actors who align with the themes of their projects. By ensuring that endorsements feel genuine and relatable, you create a stronger bond with your audience, increasing the likelihood of engagement and support.

Once you have identified potential endorsers, it's essential to establish a mutually beneficial relationship. Instead of viewing endorsements as a one-sided transaction, focus on creating a partnership that provides value to both parties. This could involve co-creating content that showcases the endorser's connection to your work or organizing promotional events that highlight both brands. For instance, a music artist could partner with a well-known fashion brand to design exclusive merchandise, enhancing visibility for both entities while appealing to a shared fan base.

In the age of social media, leveraging endorsements through digital platforms is more impactful than ever. Influencers and celebrities can amplify your message to their followers, effectively expanding your audience.

Develop a strategic social media plan that utilizes the endorser's platform for promotional campaigns. This could involve live streams, behind-the-scenes content, or collaborative posts that highlight the endorsement.

Engaging your audience through interactive content can also foster a sense of community and belonging, which is particularly effective in the entertainment sector.

Lastly, integrating endorsements into event marketing can elevate your visibility during crucial promotional periods, such as film premieres or album launches.

Consider inviting endorsers to your events, as their presence can draw media attention and increase attendance. Additionally, crafting a narrative around their involvement—such as sharing their personal connection to your work—can create compelling content that resonates with audiences. By strategically planning how endorsements fit into your broader marketing and branding initiatives, you can maximize their impact and leverage the power of association to build your fame in the entertainment industry.

Chapter Eight

Influencer Marketing in the Music Industry

Finding the Right Influencers

Finding the right influencers is a crucial step for musicians, artists, filmmakers, and content creators who wish to amplify their presence in the entertainment industry. Influencer marketing has become an indispensable tool for building brand awareness and engagement. The key to successful partnerships lies in identifying individuals whose audience aligns with your target demographic. This alignment ensures that your message reaches the right people, fostering genuine interest and creating opportunities for deeper connections.

When seeking influencers, it's essential to consider their niche and the type of content they create. For example, a filmmaker looking to promote an indie film should focus on influencers who specialize in film reviews, festival coverage, or entertainment news. Similarly, musicians might benefit from partnerships with influencers who have a strong following in music discovery or live concert experiences. By targeting influencers who resonate with your genre or style, you can tap into engaged audiences that are more likely to appreciate and promote your work.

Engagement metrics, such as likes, shares, comments, and follower growth, provide valuable insights into an influencer's effectiveness. A high follower count alone is not indicative of influence; it's crucial to examine how active and engaged their audience is. Tools like social media analytics platforms can help assess these metrics. Look for influencers who not only have a strong following but also foster a community that interacts with their content. This engagement can translate into authentic promotion and increased visibility for your project.

In addition to reach and engagement, consider the influencer's values and brand alignment. Collaborating with someone who shares your vision and ethos can create a more authentic partnership. For instance, if your film addresses social issues, an influencer known for advocacy and activism may enhance the impact of your message. Authenticity resonates with audiences, and when influencers genuinely believe in your project, their promotion will come across as sincere rather than transactional.

Lastly, building relationships with influencers often requires patience and effort. Rather than approaching them solely for promotion, consider ways to engage with them meaningfully. Interact with their content, share their work, and express genuine appreciation for what they do. This groundwork can lead to a more fruitful collaboration, where influencers feel valued and motivated to support your project. By investing time in finding the right influencers and nurturing those relationships, you can significantly enhance your visibility and success within the competitive landscape of the entertainment industry.

Building Authentic Relationships

Building authentic relationships is a cornerstone of success in the entertainment industry, especially for musicians, artists, filmmakers, influencers, and content creators. In a landscape often characterized by superficial connections and fleeting interactions, cultivating genuine relationships can set you apart and serve as a powerful vehicle for your career. Authentic connections can lead to meaningful collaborations, increased visibility, and lasting support from peers and audiences alike. This subchapter will explore key strategies for building and maintaining these relationships in a way that enhances your brand and professional journey.

The foundation of any authentic relationship is trust. In the entertainment industry, this means being transparent about your intentions, whether you're seeking partnerships, collaborations, or simply networking. Always approach others with sincerity and respect their time and contributions. When reaching out to fellow creators or potential partners, take the time to personalize your communications. Reference specific projects of theirs that resonate with you, and articulate how a collaboration could provide mutual benefits. By showing that you are genuinely interested in their work, you create a fertile ground for trust and respect to flourish.

Networking events and social media platforms offer unique opportunities to foster relationships, but they should be approached with a mindset focused on building connections rather than merely promoting oneself. Engage actively in conversations, both online and offline, by asking questions and sharing insights that reflect your knowledge of the industry. When attending events like music festivals or film premieres, seek to connect with others beyond brief pleasantries. Follow up with new acquaintances through direct messages or emails, referencing your initial conversation to remind them of your connection. This follow- up not only reinforces your interest but also demonstrates your commitment to nurturing the relationship.

Collaboration is another vital component of building authentic relationships. By working together on projects, you can deepen connections and create shared experiences that contribute to both parties' growth. Seek out opportunities for joint ventures, whether it's co-creating content, cross- promoting each other's work, or engaging in charitable initiatives.

Collaborative efforts can amplify your reach and introduce you to new audiences, while also solidifying bonds with fellow creators. Remember, the entertainment industry thrives on partnerships; your willingness to collaborate can open doors that may otherwise remain closed.

Finally, nurturing relationships requires ongoing effort and genuine engagement. Stay connected with your network by sharing their achievements and celebrating their milestones on social media or in personal interactions. Offer help when you can, whether it's providing feedback on a project or sharing insights that may benefit them. Authenticity is sustained through consistent and meaningful interactions, which can lead to a supportive community that champions your work. By investing time and energy into these relationships, you not only enhance your presence within the entertainment industry but also cultivate a network that can uplift and propel your career forward.

25 Tips on How to Find Influencers to Help Build Your Brand and Why It's Important

1. **Define Your Brand's Goals and Target Audience**
   Why: Before seeking influencers, it's crucial to understand your brand's goals and the audience you want to reach. This ensures that the influencers you choose align with your objectives and resonate with your target market.

2. **Research Your Competitors' Collaborations**
   Why: Analyzing which influencers your competitors are working with can give you insights into effective partnerships. This can help you identify similar influencers who can also enhance your brand's visibility.

3. **Use Influencer Marketing Platforms**
   Why: Platforms like Upfluence, AspireIQ, and BuzzSumo offer databases of influencers across various niches, making it easier to find the right match for your brand based on demographics, reach, and engagement.

4. **Leverage Social Media Hashtags**
   Why: Searching popular hashtags related to your industry on platforms like Instagram and Twitter can help you discover in-

fluencers who are already engaging with your niche audience. Hashtags can lead you to influencers with relevant content and followers.

5. **Consider Micro-Influencers**

   Why: Micro-influencers, typically with 10,000 to 100,000 followers, often have higher engagement rates and more loyal followers than larger influencers. They are also more cost-effective and can help build authentic connections with your audience.

6. **Check Influencer Engagement Rates**

   Why: An influencer with a high number of followers doesn't necessarily mean they have a strong impact. Tools like HypeAuditor or SocialBlade allow you to analyze engagement rates, ensuring the influencer actively interacts with their audience.

7. **Focus on Authenticity**

   Why: Consumers are more likely to trust influencers who genuinely use and enjoy the products they promote. Look for influencers whose content feels authentic and who are likely to resonate with your brand's values.

8. **Utilize Google Alerts**

   Why: Setting up Google Alerts for your industry's keywords can help you identify influencers who are generating buzz in your niche. This way, you stay informed about new and emerging voices that can benefit your brand.

9. **Use LinkedIn for B2B Influencers**

   Why: If your brand operates in a B2B space, LinkedIn is a powerful tool for finding industry experts and thought leaders who can influence your target audience. Use LinkedIn's search features to connect with potential influencers in your field.

10. **Engage with Influencers Before Reaching Out**

    Why: Building a relationship with influencers before formally reaching out can increase the chances of collaboration. Like, comment, and share their content to show genuine interest in their work.

11. **Analyze Influencer Content Quality**
Why: High-quality content reflects positively on your brand. Look for influencers who consistently produce visually appealing, well-written, and engaging content. This ensures your brand is represented in the best light.

12. **Use YouTube for Video Influencers**
Why: YouTube is a hub for video content creators who can produce in-depth reviews, tutorials, and other engaging formats. Use YouTube's search features and tools like TubeBuddy to find influencers in your industry.

13. **Find Niche Communities on Reddit**
Why: Reddit is home to niche communities where industry influencers often emerge. By participating in relevant subreddits, you can identify key voices who influence conversations and trends in your space.

14. **Leverage Influencer Marketing Agencies**
Why: Influencer marketing agencies specialize in connecting brands with influencers.

Agencies like Viral Nation or The Influencer Marketing Factory can help match you with the right influencers based on your goals and budget.

15. **Look for Influencers Using Branded Content on Instagram**
Why: Instagram's branded content tags make it easier to spot influencers who are experienced in brand partnerships. These influencers are likely to have a professional approach to collaborations.

16. **Use TikTok to Discover Emerging Influencers**
Why: TikTok's algorithm promotes content based on engage-

ment, making it a great platform to discover up-and-coming influencers. Use TikTok's search function and tools like TrendTok to identify influencers with viral potential.

17. **Evaluate Influencers' Cross-Platform Presence**

Why: Influencers who have a strong presence across multiple platforms (e.g., Instagram, YouTube, TikTok) can provide more comprehensive brand exposure. Look for influencers who can amplify your message across various channels.

18. **Use Podcasts for Thought Leadership Influencers**

Why: Podcasts are a growing medium for thought leadership. Find influencers who host or appear on podcasts relevant to your industry using directories like Podchaser or Chartable.

19. **Check Influencer Transparency**

Why: Transparency is crucial for maintaining trust. Look for influencers who clearly disclose paid partnerships, as this transparency reflects well on both the influencer and your brand.

20. **Explore Pinterest for Visual Content Creators**

Why: Pinterest is a powerful platform for discovering influencers in lifestyle, fashion, home decor, and food industries. Search for influencers who create compelling visual content that aligns with your brand's aesthetic.

21. **Monitor Industry Blogs**

Why: Bloggers often have dedicated, niche audiences who trust their recommendations. Use tools like Bloglovin' or AllTop to find influential bloggers in your industry.

22. **Utilize Influencer Search Engines**

Why: Influencer search engines like Klear or Traackr allow you to filter influencers based on location, engagement, and niche, helping you narrow down the best candidates for your brand.

23. Offer Value Beyond Payment

Why: Influencers are more likely to partner with brands that offer value beyond financial compensation. Consider offering exclusive experiences, products, or long- term partnerships that align with their interests.

24. Look for Influencers Who Reflect Your Brand's Diversity

Why: Representation matters. Seek out influencers who reflect the diversity of your target audience in terms of ethnicity, gender, and lifestyle, ensuring your brand resonates with a wider range of consumers.

25. Monitor Trends and Adjust Your Strategy

Why: The influencer landscape evolves rapidly. Regularly monitor trends and adjust your strategy to stay relevant. Tools like Google Trends or Trendwatching can help you stay ahead of emerging influencer trends.

Conclusion

Finding the right influencers to build your brand is crucial because influencers have the power to connect with their audience in authentic and meaningful ways. They can amplify your message, increase brand awareness, and drive conversions. By using these 25 tips and leveraging the resources available, you can develop effective influencer partnerships that help you achieve your business goals.

Measuring the Success of Influencer Campaigns

Measuring the success of influencer campaigns is crucial for musicians, artists, filmmakers, influencers, and content creators who wish to maximize their impact in the entertainment industry. The effectiveness of these campaigns can be evaluated through various metrics, each offering insights into engagement, reach, and conversion. Understanding these metrics allows creators to refine their strategies, ensuring that they not only connect with their audiences but also achieve their specific goals, whether that's increased brand awareness, audience growth, or direct sales.

One of the most fundamental metrics to consider is engagement rate, which includes likes, shares, comments, and overall interaction with the content. High engagement levels indicate that the audience resonates with the influencer's message and the content being promoted. By assessing engagement, artists and brands can gauge how effectively the influencer communicates the desired message. This metric can also provide insights into the audience demographics, helping creators identify which segments are most responsive to their campaigns.

Reach and impressions are additional metrics that play a vital role in measuring influencer campaign success.

Reach refers to the total number of unique users who view the content, while impressions indicate the total number of times the content was displayed, regardless of whether it was clicked. For musicians and filmmakers, understanding the difference between these two metrics can help in evaluating the overall visibility of their campaigns. A high reach with low engagement may suggest that while the content is being seen, it isn't compelling enough to inspire interaction, prompting a reassessment of content strategy.

Conversions and sales tracking are also critical for gauging the success of influencer partnerships, especially in scenarios where direct action is desired. This could be in the form of downloads, ticket sales, merchandise purchases, or streaming numbers. Utilizing tools such as unique discount codes, trackable links, or dedicated landing pages can provide clear data on how many conversions result from the campaign. By analyzing these figures, creators can determine the return on investment (ROI) of their influencer marketing efforts and make informed decisions for future campaigns.

Finally, it is essential to gather qualitative feedback from both the audience and the influencers themselves. Surveys, polls, and direct communication can provide valuable insights into how the campaign was perceived and whether it achieved the desired emotional response. Understanding audience sentiment can help in refining future content and collaboration strategies, ensuring that subsequent campaigns resonate even more deeply. By combining quantitative metrics with qualitative feedback, musicians, artists, filmmakers, and content creators can create a holistic view of their influencer campaigns, enabling them to navigate the entertainment industry with greater efficacy.

Chapter Nine

Brand Integration in Film and Television

Understanding the Basics of Brand Integration

Brand integration is a strategic approach that allows creators in the entertainment industry to align their content with brands in a way that feels authentic and engaging. It goes beyond mere product placement; it involves weaving a brand's identity and values into the narrative fabric of a project, whether that's a song, film, or digital content. For musicians, filmmakers, and influencers, understanding this concept is crucial for fostering partnerships that not only enhance their visibility but also resonate with their audience. By integrating brands thoughtfully, creators can amplify their messages while offering brands an avenue to connect with a dedicated fan base.

One of the foundational aspects of brand integration is alignment. The partnership must make sense both creatively and strategically. For instance, a musician endorsing a beverage brand should ensure that the brand's image aligns with their personal ethos and the themes of their music. The integration should feel natural rather than forced; when audiences perceive authenticity, they are more likely to engage positively. This requires a deep understanding of both the creator's brand and the brands with which they wish to collaborate. Creators should evaluate potential partners based on shared values, audience demographics, and the overall narrative they wish to convey.

Another critical component of successful brand integration is storytelling. Audiences are drawn to narratives that evoke emotions or provoke thought. When a brand is integrated into a story—be it through a music video, a film scene, or a social media post—it should enhance the storyline rather than distract from it. This can involve showcasing a product in a way that complements the content's themes or using it as a plot device that adds depth to the characters. By crafting a compelling narrative around the brand, creators can transform what might be seen as a promotional effort into an engaging experience for the audience.

In addition to storytelling, the method of integration plays a significant role in its effectiveness. There are various strategies for incorporating brands into content, ranging from subtle mentions to more overt features. The choice of method should be informed by the project's tone and the target audience's preferences. For example, a documentary might benefit from a more informative approach, while a music video could embrace a more artistic expression of the brand. Understanding these nuances allows creators to tailor their integrations to suit their unique style while optimizing audience engagement.

Finally, measuring the impact of brand integration is essential for refining future partnerships and strategies. Creators should track metrics such as audience reactions, engagement rates, and even sales data where applicable. Feedback from the audience can provide valuable insights into what worked and what didn't, enabling creators to make informed decisions in their future collaborations. By continuously assessing the effectiveness of brand integration efforts, musicians, filmmakers, and content creators can not only enhance their own brand but also build lasting relationships with partners that contribute to their overall success in the entertainment industry.

10 Tips and Tools for Brand Integration in Film and Television and Why to Use Them

1. **Identify Relevant Content for Integration**

   Why: Choosing the right film or TV show that aligns with your brand's image and target audience is crucial. Brand integration should feel natural within the storyline to resonate with viewers.

   Tool: IMDB Pro helps identify upcoming productions, giving you insights into the cast, crew, and storyline to evaluate relevance for your brand.

2. **Partner with Production Companies**

   Why: Building relationships with production companies allows for early involvement in the creative process, ensuring your brand fits seamlessly into the story. This also helps in negotiating favorable terms.

   Tool: Studio System is a database that connects brands with production companies, offering contact details and information on upcoming projects.

3. **Leverage Product Placement Agencies**

   Why: Product placement agencies specialize in connecting

brands with appropriate film and TV opportunities. They help secure on-screen exposure and ensure the placement aligns with the brand's goals.

Tool: Agencies like Propaganda GEM and BEN (Branded Entertainment Network) have expertise in brand integration and can facilitate partnerships.

4. **Focus on Subtlety and Authenticity**
Why: Overt or forced brand integrations can turn viewers off. Subtle placements that feel authentic to the storyline are more likely to be well-received and effective in boosting brand recall.

Tool: StoryFit uses AI to analyze scripts and recommend natural points for brand integration, ensuring the placement feels organic within the story.

5. **Negotiate Long-Term Partnerships**
Why: Long-term brand integrations across multiple episodes or films can lead to stronger brand recall and deeper audience connection. Consistent exposure is key to reinforcing your brand message.

Tool: Greenlight Rights helps negotiate and manage long-term brand partnerships within entertainment properties, ensuring consistency and compliance.

6. **Consider Digital and Streaming Platforms**
Why: With the rise of streaming platforms, digital integration offers new opportunities for brands to reach audiences on platforms like Netflix, Hulu, and YouTube Originals. These platforms often provide data- driven insights to target specific demographics.

Tool: Tubular Labs offers analytics on digital video content, helping brands understand the performance of their integrations on streaming platforms.

7. Create Multi-Channel Campaigns

Why: Brand integration should extend beyond the screen. By creating multi- channel campaigns that tie in with the film or TV show, such as social media promotions or in-store activations, you can maximize impact and audience engagement.

Tool: Hootsuite enables the management of multi-channel campaigns by scheduling and tracking posts across social media platforms to complement your brand's on-screen presence.

8. Involve Celebrities in the Campaign

Why: If a celebrity associated with the film or show promotes your brand, it adds credibility and enhances audience connection.

Collaborating with actors on branded content outside of the production can amplify the integration's impact.

Tool: Captiv8 helps brands connect with influencers and celebrities, facilitating partnerships that go beyond the screen.

9. Measure Effectiveness with Data Analytics

Why: Tracking the success of your brand integration through data analytics ensures you understand its impact. Analyzing metrics like brand recall, audience reach, and engagement helps refine future integration strategies.

Tool: Nielsen Brand Effect provides data on the effectiveness of brand placements in films and TV, offering insights into audience engagement and brand lift.

10. Create Interactive or Second-Screen Experiences

Why: Engaging audiences with second-screen experiences during or after the content is consumed adds an interactive element to your brand integration, deepening engagement and extending the impact.

Tool: Shazam for Brands enables second-screen interactions by allowing viewers to use the Shazam app to access exclusive content or promotions related to your brand integration during the show or film.

Conclusion

Brand integration in film and television is a powerful marketing strategy that can elevate your brand's visibility and credibility. By strategically placing your brand within entertainment content, you can connect with audiences in an organic and memorable way. Using these tools and tips ensures that your integration efforts are targeted, authentic, and measurable, maximizing the return on investment for your brand.

Developing Partnerships with Producers and Directors

Developing partnerships with producers and directors is a strategic move for musicians, artists, filmmakers, influencers, and content creators looking to enhance their visibility and credibility in the entertainment industry. Collaborations with established figures in the film and television space can open doors to new audiences and opportunities, allowing you to leverage their expertise and networks. Understanding the dynamics of these partnerships is crucial for maximizing their potential and ensuring mutual benefit.

To begin, it's essential to identify producers and directors whose work aligns with your artistic vision and brand. Research their past projects, paying attention to their style, themes, and audience demographics. This alignment is critical, as it ensures that any collaboration will resonate with both your fan base and theirs. Once you've identified potential partners, consider reaching out with a personalized pitch that highlights not only your work but also the unique value you can bring to their projects. This might include your existing audience, a distinctive artistic perspective, or innovative ideas for integrating your work into their films or shows.

Networking plays a pivotal role in forming these partnerships. Attend industry events, film festivals, and workshops to meet producers and directors in person. Engaging in conversations and showcasing your work in these settings can help you build rapport and trust. Furthermore, consider utilizing social media platforms to connect with industry professionals. Engaging with their content, sharing insights, and expressing genuine interest in their projects can create organic opportunities for collaboration. Remember, relationships take time to cultivate, so patience and persistence are key.

Once a partnership is established, clear communication is vital. Define roles, expectations, and deliverables from the outset to avoid misunderstandings later on. Discuss how your collaboration will be marketed and what promotional strategies will be employed to reach wider audiences. For instance, if you're a musician collaborating on a film, consider how your music can be integrated into the film's marketing campaign. This could involve exclusive behind-the-scenes content, social media takeovers, or even live performances at film premieres, all of which can amplify both your reach and the film's visibility.

Finally, evaluate the outcomes of your partnership to inform future collaborations. Analyze engagement metrics, audience feedback, and overall impact on your branding and marketing goals. This reflection will not only help you understand what worked well but also provide valuable insights for approaching future projects. Building strong partnerships with producers and directors is an ongoing process that can significantly enhance your standing in the entertainment industry, making it essential to approach each collaboration with strategic intent and a focus on long-term growth.

Case Studies: Successful Brand Integrations

In the rapidly evolving landscape of the entertainment industry, successful brand integrations have become a cornerstone of marketing strategies for musicians, filmmakers, influencers, and content creators. These integrations not only enhance visibility and revenue but also help establish a deeper connection with audiences. By examining noteworthy case studies, we can glean valuable insights into how effective collaborations between brands and creators can lead to mutual success. This subchapter explores several exemplary cases that demonstrate the power of strategic partnerships.

One prominent example is the collaboration between the popular television series "Stranger Things" and various brands during its promotional campaigns.

The nostalgic aesthetic of the show appealed to both millennials and Generation Z, making it an ideal platform for brands like Eggo and Coca-Cola to align themselves with the show's themes. The integration of Eggo waffles into the storyline became iconic, sparking a surge in sales for the brand. Coca-Cola capitalized on the 1980s theme by re-releasing its classic cans, creating a buzz that resonated with the show's audience. This case illustrates how a well- executed brand integration can enhance narrative depth while driving consumer engagement.

Another successful case can be found in the music industry, where artists like Travis Scott have effectively fused their brand with major corporations. Scott's collaboration with McDonald's in 2020 exemplifies this trend. The partnership resulted in the launch of the "Travis Scott Meal," which was not only a marketing success but also a cultural phenomenon. The combination of Scott's music, social media influence, and McDonald's widespread reach created a unique synergy that resonated with fans, leading to increased sales for the fast-food giant and heightened visibility for Scott's music. This case highlights how leveraging an artist's personal brand can amplify a corporate campaign while providing authentic content that appeals to a shared audience.

In the realm of film, the integration of brands within the narratives of movies has proven effective for both storytelling and marketing. A notable instance is the partnership between Ford and the "Transformers" franchise. The film series featured Ford vehicles prominently, aligning the brand with the action- packed, adventurous spirit of the movies. This strategic placement not only reinforced Ford's image but also reached millions of viewers, enhancing brand recognition and customer loyalty. The seamless integration of products into the storyline demonstrates how films can serve as powerful platforms for brand visibility, while also providing audiences with a sense of realism and relatability.

Social media strategy has also played a pivotal role in successful brand integrations. Influencer marketing is particularly effective in creating authentic connections between brands and audiences. For instance, YouTube star James Charles' collaboration with Morphe Cosmetics showcased the potential of influencer partnerships. By co-creating a makeup palette, Charles not only bolstered Morphe's brand image but also tapped into his dedicated fanbase to drive product sales. This case exemplifies how influencers can leverage their platforms to create innovative marketing campaigns that resonate deeply with their followers while providing brands with a powerful avenue for engagement.

These case studies illustrate the dynamic interplay between brands and creators in the entertainment industry. By understanding the intricacies of successful brand integrations, musicians, artists, filmmakers, and influencers can craft their own strategies that resonate with their audiences. Whether through strategic partnerships, product placements, or influencer collaborations, the potential for success lies in the ability to forge authentic connections that enhance both the creator's narrative and the brand's message. As the industry continues to evolve, the lessons learned from these examples will be invaluable for anyone seeking to navigate the complex terrain of publicity and marketing without the aid of traditional publicists.

Chapter Ten

Digital Marketing Strategies for Indie Films

Building an Online Presence

Building an online presence is a crucial step for any musician, artist, filmmaker, influencer, or content creator aiming to establish themselves in the competitive entertainment industry. In today's digital landscape, the internet serves as a primary vehicle for promotion, engagement, and brand development. A well-crafted online presence allows creatives to connect with their audience, showcase their work, and create opportunities for collaboration and growth. This subchapter will explore essential strategies for building and maintaining a robust online identity that resonates with your target audience.

The foundation of a solid online presence lies in several key platforms, including social media, personal websites, and streaming services. Social media platforms such as Instagram, TikTok, Twitter, and Facebook provide immediate access to potential fans and collaborators. Each platform has its unique strengths; for instance, Instagram is ideal for visual artists and musicians to showcase their work, while TikTok offers a dynamic space for short, engaging video content. A personal website serves as your digital portfolio, where you can centralize your work, share your story, and provide contact information for opportunities. Additionally, leveraging streaming services like Spotify or YouTube can amplify your reach, allowing you to distribute your content directly to a global audience.

Consistency is key when building an online presence. Regularly posting content that reflects your brand identity helps maintain audience engagement and interest. Establishing a content calendar can help you plan and organize your posts, ensuring that you deliver fresh, relevant material consistently. This could include behind-the-scenes glimpses of your creative process, updates on new projects, or interactive content such as polls and Q&A sessions.

By creating a predictable rhythm in your content delivery, you foster a sense of community and anticipation among your followers, which can lead to increased loyalty and support.

25 Digital Marketing Strategies for Indie Films for Building an Online Presence

1. **Create a Dedicated Film Website**
   Why: A dedicated website acts as the central hub for your film's marketing. Include information about the film, trailers, cast bios, press kits, and screening schedules. This ensures that potential viewers, press, and collaborators can easily find information.

   Tool: Wix or Squarespaceare user-friendly platforms that allow you to create a professional-looking website quickly.

2. **Leverage Social Media Platforms**
   Why: Social media is essential for building a following, engaging with fans, and sharing updates. Platforms like Instagram, Facebook, Twitter, and TikTok allow you to connect directly with your audience.

   Tool: Hootsuite helps manage and schedule posts across multiple social media platforms, keeping your marketing consistent.

3. **Engage with Film Communities on Reddit**
   Why: Reddit has active communities focused on independent films, filmmaking, and cinema. Engaging in these subreddits can

help you build awareness and gain feedback.

Tool: Reddit itself is the tool and popular subreddits include r/Filmmakers r/indiefilm and r/movies.

4. Create Teaser Trailers and Clips

Why: Short, engaging teaser trailers and clips build anticipation and excitement for your film. Regularly releasing content keeps your film on the audience's radar.

Tool: Adobe Premiere Pro for editing high-quality trailers and clips that can be shared across platforms.

5. Start a Crowdfunding Campaign

Why: Crowdfunding not only helps raise funds but also builds a community around your film. Supporters of your campaign are likely to become advocates and help promote your film.

Tool: Kickstarter or Indiegogo are popular platforms that allow you to raise funds and engage with your audience simultaneously.

6. Collaborate with Influencers

Why: Partnering with influencers or film bloggers can expand your reach. Influencers with an audience that matches your target demographic can help create buzz and attract attention to your film.

Tool: AspireIQ or Influencity can help you find relevant influencers for your film's genre and audience.

7. Use Email Marketing

Why: Building an email list allows you to keep fans and industry professionals informed about your film's progress, release dates, and exclusive content. Email campaigns are a direct way to reach your audience.

Tool: Mailchimp or Constant Contact offer easy-to-use platforms for creating and managing email campaigns.

8. **Submit to Film Festivals**
   Why: Film festivals can provide exposure, reviews, and a platform for distribution deals. Building a festival presence boosts your film's credibility and offers networking opportunities.

   Tool: FilmFreeway or Withoutabox allow you to discover and submit your indie film to festivals worldwide

9. **Leverage Facebook and Instagram Ads**
   Why: Paid social media advertising can help target specific demographics. Running ads on Facebook and Instagram can increase your film's visibility and attract potential viewers.

   Tool: Facebook Ads Manager allows you to create and manage ad campaigns across Facebook and Instagram, targeting audiences based on their interests and behavior.

10. **Engage in Content Marketing**
    Why: Write blog posts, create behind-the-scenes videos, or share interviews with the cast and crew. Content marketing provides additional value to your audience and keeps them engaged with your film over time.

    Tool: Medium or your film's blog can be used to publish written content that tells your film's story in more depth.

11. **Optimize Your Website for SEO**
    Why: Search engine optimization (SEO) ensures your film's website appears in search results. Proper SEO makes it easier for people to find your film when searching for related topics online.

    Tool: Yoast SEO for WordPress helps optimize your website's

content for search engines, improving your film's visibility.

12. **Engage Fans with User-Generated Content**
Why: Encouraging fans to create content related to your film—whether it's artwork, fan theories, or reviews—can help spread the word organically. Sharing this content boosts engagement and community-building.

Tool: Use platforms like Instagram or TikTok to run contests or challenges that encourage fan participation.

13. **Start a YouTube Channel**
Why: YouTube is an excellent platform for sharing trailers, be-hind- the-scenes footage, and interviews. It's also the sec-ond-largest search engine, making it a key platform for visibility.

Tool: YouTube Studio helps you manage your channel, optimize videos for SEO, and analyze viewer engagement.

14. **Use Google Ads**
Why: Google Ads allows you to target specific keywords, ensuring that people searching for related films or topics discover your movie. Paid search ads can drive traffic to your website or landing page.

Tool: Google Ads provides comprehensive tools for creating and managing pay-per-click campaigns based on specific search queries.

15. **Create an Interactive Website Experience**
Why: Adding interactive elements like quizzes, polls, or games can make your film's website more engaging, encouraging visi-tors to spend more time and explore further.

Tool: Use tools like Typeform or Outgrow to create interactive quizzes or experiences that relate to your film's themes or storyline.

16. **Build Partnerships with Niche Blogs**
Why: Reach out to niche bloggers who cover independent films or your film's genre. A review or interview featured on their blog can introduce your film to a targeted audience.

Tool: Use tools like BuzzStream to find and manage relationships with bloggers who align with your film's target audience.

17. **Host Virtual Screenings**
Why: Virtual screenings make it easy to reach a global audience, especially for indie films without wide distribution. They allow fans to watch your film from the comfort of their homes while engaging in live Q&A sessions.

Tool: Platforms like Vimeo On Demand or Eventive provide tools for hosting and monetizing virtual film screenings.

18. **Run a Contest or Giveaway**
Why: Contests and giveaways can generate buzz and increase your following. Offering exclusive merchandise, free tickets, or behind- the-scenes experiences incentivizes participation.

Tool: Use Gleam or Rafflecopter to run social media contests that boost engagement and promote your film.

19. **Create a Podcast Around Your Film**
Why: Podcasts provide a platform to discuss your film's themes, production process, or related topics. A podcast can serve as an additional channel for reaching potential viewers and creating a deeper connection.

Tool: Anchor or Buzzsprout make it easy to record, distribute, and promote your podcast across multiple platforms.

20. **Optimize for Mobile**

Why: With so much content consumed on mobile devices, ensure that your website, social media profiles, and videos are mobile-friendly. A seamless mobile experience increases engagement and keeps your audience on your content longer.

Tool: Google's Mobile-Friendly Test allows you to check your website's mobile optimization and make improvements if needed.

21. **Collaborate with Local Businesses**

Why: Partnering with local businesses can expand your film's reach. Local coffee shops, bookstores, or theaters may be willing to promote your film in exchange for cross-promotion.

Tool: Canva allows you to design eye-catching posters, flyers, and promotional materials to distribute in local venues.

22. **Leverage Email Sign-Up Popups**

Why: Adding email sign-up popups to your website helps you grow your email list by capturing interested visitors. This allows you to nurture leads with updates, exclusive content, and ticket sales.

Tool: OptinMonster helps you create customizable email sign-up popups and forms for your website.

23. **Engage with Industry Influencers on LinkedIn**

Why: LinkedIn is a valuable platform for networking with film industry professionals, from distributors to media outlets. Engaging with relevant content or joining groups can boost your film's credibility and expand your network.

Tool: LinkedIn Sales Navigator allows you to find and connect with industry professionals who can help promote your film.

24. **Invest in Retargeting Ads**

Why: Retargeting ads show your film to people who have visited your website or engaged with your content before but didn't take action. These ads serve as reminders and can help convert potential viewers.

Tool: Google Display Network or Facebook Pixel can be used to set up retargeting campaigns that bring visitors back to your website.

25. **Submit Your Film to Online Databases**

Why: Listing your film on popular online databases increases its visibility and makes it more discoverable by fans, critics, and industry professionals. These listings often rank highly in search engine results.

Tool: Submit to IMDb and Rotten Tomatoes to ensure your film is represented on platforms where potential viewers look for information.

Conclusion

By combining these 25 digital marketing strategies, indie filmmakers can build a robust online presence, generate buzz, and attract a wider audience. From leveraging social media and email marketing to collaborating with influencers and local businesses, each strategy helps promote your film and engage with potential viewers in a meaningful way.

In addition to consistency and using these 25 digital marketing strategies, authenticity plays a vital role in establishing a genuine connection with your audience. Today's consumers are increasingly discerning and gravitate towards creators who exhibit vulnerability and relatability. Sharing personal stories, challenges, and triumphs can humanize your brand and make your audience feel invested in your journey. Engaging with your audience through comments, direct messages, and live sessions demonstrates that you value their input and feedback, further solidifying their connection to your work.

Finally, consider the potential for collaborations and partnerships to expand your online presence.

Collaborating with other artists, influencers, or brands can introduce you to new audiences and enhance your credibility. Whether through joint projects, guest appearances, or social media takeovers, these partnerships can create mutual benefits and amplify your reach. Additionally, exploring celebrity endorsements and brand integrations can help elevate your profile within the entertainment industry, provided that the collaborations align with your artistic vision and values.

By strategically enhancing your online presence through these avenues, you can effectively navigate the complexities of the entertainment landscape and cultivate a thriving career.

Crowdfunding and its Marketing Potential

Crowdfunding has emerged as a powerful tool for musicians, artists, filmmakers, influencers, and content creators, enabling them to secure funding directly from their audience. Unlike traditional funding models, which often rely on large investors or studio backing, crowdfunding allows creators to engage with their supporters on a personal level. This method not only provides the necessary financial backing but also serves as a marketing strategy that fosters community and loyalty among fans. By leveraging platforms like Kickstarter, Indiegogo, and Patreon, creators can transform their projects into collective endeavors, inviting their audience to be part of the journey from the very beginning.

One of the most significant advantages of crowdfunding is the ability to gauge market interest before fully committing to a project. By promoting a crowdfunding campaign, creators can assess the demand for their work, refine their offerings based on feedback, and build a dedicated fanbase in the process. This direct interaction with potential supporters allows for the cultivation of an engaged audience, which is invaluable in today's entertainment landscape. The marketing potential lies not only in the funds raised but also in the exposure gained through the campaign itself, as creators can utilize social media and other digital marketing strategies to spread the word.

Effective marketing strategies are essential for a successful crowdfunding campaign. Creators must craft compelling narratives that resonate with their target audience, highlighting the unique aspects of their project and the impact of their work. This storytelling approach not only captivates potential backers but also encourages sharing across social media platforms, thereby amplifying visibility.

Employing influencer marketing can also enhance outreach, as collaborating with established figures in the industry can lend credibility and attract a wider audience. By creating visually appealing promotional materials and leveraging the power of social proof, creators can significantly boost their chances of reaching their crowdfunding goals.

Additionally, crowdfunding offers opportunities for merchandise branding and exclusive rewards, which can further enhance marketing efforts. By providing backers with unique incentives—such as limited- edition merchandise or behind-the-scenes access— creators can create a sense of urgency and exclusivity that drives contributions. This approach not only raises funds but also strengthens the brand identity of the creator, making them more recognizable in the industry. Moreover, the feedback and interaction with supporters during the campaign can lead to valuable insights about audience preferences, allowing creators to refine their future marketing strategies.

In conclusion, crowdfunding is not just a means of financing; it is a multifaceted marketing tool that can elevate a creator's visibility and engagement within the entertainment industry. By integrating effective storytelling, leveraging social media strategies, and offering unique rewards, musicians, artists, filmmakers, and influencers can maximize the potential of their crowdfunding campaigns. As the landscape of enter-tainment continues to evolve, embracing crowdfunding as a strategic marketing approach can empower creators to navigate their careers with greater autonomy and success.

Engaging with Film Communities Online

Engaging with film communities online has become an essential strategy for musicians, filmmakers, influencers, and content creators looking to enhance their visibility and establish meaningful connections within the entertainment industry. As the digital landscape continues to evolve, it offers a plethora of platforms where individuals can showcase their work, share insights, and collaborate with like-minded creatives. By actively participating in these communities, you can not only bolster your brand but also tap into a network that can amplify your reach and influence.

One of the most effective ways to engage with film communities online is through social media platforms. Sites like Instagram, Twitter, and Facebook host vibrant groups and pages dedicated to film enthusiasts, filmmakers, and content creators. By joining these groups, you can share your projects, solicit feedback, and promote your work to an audience that is genuinely interested in film and media. Additionally, utilizing hashtags related to your niche can help you discover and connect with potential collaborators and fans who share your passion.

Participating in forums like Reddit or specialized film discussion boards can also be beneficial. Engaging in thoughtful discussions about current trends, industry challenges, or specific films can position you as an informed and active member of the community. By providing valuable insights and contributing to conversations, you not only showcase your expertise but also build credibility, making it more likely that others will be interested in your work. This approach fosters organic connections that can lead to collaborations, partnerships, and audience growth.

Another vital aspect of engaging with film communities is attending virtual events such as webinars, film festivals, and online workshops. Many of these events have shifted online, allowing for greater accessibility and participation. By attending these gatherings, you can network with industry professionals, learn from experts, and gain exposure to new trends and technologies. Engaging with attendees through Q&A sessions, chat features, or social media during these events can significantly expand your network and create opportunities for future projects.

25 Online Film Communities To Join And Gain Publicity From

1. **IndieTalk**

   Description: A forum for independent filmmakers to discuss production, post-production, distribution, and more. It offers advice and networking opportunities for indie filmmakers.

   Website: indietalk.com

2. **Stage 32**

   Description: A global network for filmmakers, actors, and other entertainment professionals. It provides education, networking opportunities, and job postings within the industry.

   Website: stage32.com

3. **Filmmaker Forum**

   Description: A community for filmmakers to discuss everything from screenwriting and cinematography to editing and distribution. It's a hub for sharing resources and experiences.

   Website: filmmakerforum.org

4. **No Film School**

   Description: A resource and community site for independent

filmmakers, offering articles, tutorials, and discussion boards on various filmmaking topics.

Website: nofilmschool.com

5. DVXuser

Description: A forum focused on digital video production and cinematography. It's a great resource for filmmakers interested in camera gear, editing software, and production techniques.

Website: dvxuser.com

6. r/Filmmakers (Reddit)

Description: A subreddit where filmmakers of all levels can ask questions, share their work, and get feedback from the Reddit film community.

Website: reddit.com/r/Filmmakers

7. Film Riot Community

Description: A community tied to the Film Riot YouTube channel, which focuses on indie filmmaking tips, tutorials, and discussions. The forum allows for deeper engagement with other filmmakers.

Website: community.filmriot.com

8. Create COW

Description: A massive forum and resource hub for professionals in film, video, and VFX. It covers a wide range of technical and creative topics, from editing software to visual effects.

Website: creativecow.net

9. Shooting People

Description: An online network for indie filmmakers in the UK and beyond. It helps filmmakers connect, collaborate, and share resources, with daily bulletins and casting calls.

Website: shootingpeople.org

10. **Filmmakers Network (FMN)**
Description: A networking community focused on connecting filmmakers with opportunities, collaborators, and industry insights. It includes a wide range of forums on different aspects of filmmaking.

Website: filmmakersnetwork.org

11. **The D-Word**
Description: A global online community specifically for documentary filmmakers. It offers a platform to discuss all aspects of documentary filmmaking, from funding to distribution.

Website: d-word.com

12. **Sundance Collab**
Description: An extension of the Sundance Institute, Co//ab offers online courses, events, and a global community for filmmakers, writers, and creators. It's a space to learn and connect with peers.

Website: collab.sundance.org

13. **Filmmaker's Alliance**
Description: An online community that supports independent filmmakers with resources, funding opportunities, and advice. The site focuses on building relationships and providing educational content.

Website: filmmakersalliance.org

14. **Raindance**
Description: A global platform for indie filmmakers offering on-line courses, resources, and a vibrant community. It's also known for hosting the Raindance Film Festival.

Website: raindance.org

15. **New Filmmakers LA (NFMLA)**
Description: A non-profit organization that provides emerging filmmakers with a supportive network. NFMLA hosts monthly screenings and offers networking events, workshops, and panels.

Website: nfmla.org

16. **Filmmaker IQ**
Description: An educational resource and community focused on the art, history, and science of filmmaking. It provides in-depth tutorials and a forum for filmmakers to discuss techniques.

Website: filmmakeriq.com

17. **Film Industry Network**
Description: An international online community offering news, industry insights, and a platform for filmmakers to share and promote their work. It's a space for networking and industry news.

Website: filmindustry.network

18. **Screencraft**
Description: Known for its screenplay competitions, ScreenCraft also offers a community space for writers and filmmakers to connect, share advice, and collaborate on projects.

Website: screencraft.org

19. **The Black and Blue**
Description: A community and resource hub for camera assistants, cinematographers, and anyone interested in the technical side of filmmaking. The site offers guides, tips, and community support.

Website: theblackandblue.com

20. **CineD (formerly Cinema5D)**
Description: A community and news platform for filmmakers and cinematographers, focusing on gear reviews, industry news, and educational content related to filmmaking technology.

Website: cined.com

21. **Cinematic Arts Community**
Description: A private community for filmmakers and creators on Discord, where members can discuss various aspects of filmmaking, share their projects, and receive feedback.

Website: Discord, invite-based, often linked via larger filmmaking groups.

22. **The Film Collaborative**
Description: A non-profit organization dedicated to helping independent filmmakers with distribution, festival strategy, and marketing. Their community offers resources and advice to navigate the film industry.

Website: thefilmcollaborative.org

23. **Moviemaker Community**
Description: An extension of the MovieMaker Magazine, this community offers advice, articles, and discussions on filmmaking, screenwriting, and the film industry at large.

Website: moviemaker.com

24. **Filmmaker Junction**

Description: A Facebook group that serves as a community for filmmakers to share tips, seek advice, and connect with others in the industry. It's a casual space for indie filmmakers and creatives.

Website: Facebook Group (Search "Filmmaker Junction")

25. **Women in Film & Television (WIFT)**

Description: An international organization that supports women in the film and television industries. WIFT provides networking opportunities, mentorship, and resources to women filmmakers and professionals.

Website: wiftn.org (Various chapters worldwide)

Conclusion

These online film communities provide a wide range of resources, networking opportunities, and educational content for filmmakers at every level. Whether you're looking for technical advice, industry insights, or collaboration opportunities, these communities are valuable tools for building connections and advancing your filmmaking career.

Ultimately, the key to successfully engaging with film communities online lies in authenticity and consistency. Share not just your successes but also your creative process, challenges, and lessons learned along the way. By being transparent and approachable, you cultivate a loyal following that resonates with your journey. As you continue to build relationships within these communities, remember that collaboration is at the heart of the entertainment industry; the more you engage, the more you'll find doors opening for new opportunities and connections that can propel your career forward.

Chapter Eleven

Merchandise Branding for Music Artists and Bands

Creating Compelling Merchandise

Creating compelling merchandise is an essential aspect of building a brand in the entertainment industry. For musicians, artists, filmmakers, influencers, and content creators, merchandise serves not only as a revenue stream but also as a vital tool for branding and audience engagement. In a saturated market, standing out requires thoughtful design, unique offerings, and a deep understanding of your audience's preferences. This subchapter delves into the strategic elements that make merchandise resonate with consumers and enhance your overall brand identity.

First, understanding your target audience is crucial when developing merchandise. Conducting surveys, engaging with fans on social media, and analyzing purchase behaviors can provide insights into what your audience values and desires. For instance, musicians might find that their fans are more inclined towards limited-edition vinyl records or exclusive merchandise that reflects their music's aesthetic. Similarly, filmmakers can create merchandise that ties into their film's themes, such as behind-the-scenes photos or signed scripts. By aligning your merchandise with your audience's interests, you can foster a deeper emotional connection and encourage loyalty to your brand.

Design plays a pivotal role in creating compelling merchandise. The visual appeal of your products can significantly influence purchasing decisions.

Collaborating with skilled graphic designers or artists can help ensure that your merchandise reflects your brand's ethos and aesthetics. High-quality materials and thoughtful packaging also enhance the perception of your products, making them more desirable. Consider launching themed merchandise around specific projects or events to create buzz and excitement, thereby increasing interest and sales. Limited editions or seasonal drops can also encourage urgency among fans, prompting them to act quickly to secure unique items.

Marketing your merchandise effectively is just as important as its creation. Utilize social media platforms to showcase your products through captivating visuals and storytelling. Engaging content, such as behind-the- scenes videos of the design process or testimonials from fans, can drive interest and highlight the value of your merchandise. Collaborating with influencers or fellow creators can also amplify your reach, as their endorsement can lend credibility and attract new customers. Implementing strategic timing for product launches—such as aligning them with album releases, film premieres, or special events—can further optimize visibility and sales.

Finally, an essential component of successful merchandise is creating a seamless purchasing experience. Ensure that your online store is user-friendly, with easy navigation and secure payment options.

Consider offering bundles or discounts for fans who purchase multiple items, which can increase overall sales. Additionally, integrating merchandise promotions into your digital marketing strategies, such as email newsletters or live streams, can enhance engagement and drive traffic to your store. By prioritizing both the creation and promotion of compelling merchandise, you can strengthen your brand in the entertainment industry and cultivate a loyal fan base that supports your creative endeavors.

Strategies for Selling Merchandise Online

When it comes to selling merchandise online, musicians, artists, filmmakers, and influencers must adopt strategic approaches that combine creativity with a keen understanding of their target audience. The first essential strategy is building a robust online presence. This involves creating a visually appealing website that serves as a central hub for your merchandise. High-quality images, engaging product descriptions, and easy navigation are crucial. Additionally, integrating e-commerce functionalities, such as secure payment gateways and user-friendly checkout processes, can significantly enhance the shopping experience, encouraging fans to make purchases rather than abandon their carts.

Leveraging social media platforms is another vital strategy to promote merchandise effectively. Each platform offers unique opportunities for engagement and sales. For instance, Instagram's visual nature makes it ideal for showcasing merchandise through eye-catching posts and stories. Utilizing features such as shoppable posts can simplify the purchasing process for followers.

Additionally, hosting live streams or Q&A sessions where you can showcase new products allows for real-time interaction with fans, creating a sense of exclusivity and urgency. Engaging with your audience through polls or feedback requests can help tailor your merchandise offerings to their preferences, fostering a deeper connection with your brand.

Collaborations and partnerships can also play a significant role in expanding your merchandise reach. Teaming up with other artists, influencers, or brands can introduce your products to new audiences. Whether through co-branded merchandise or cross-promotional campaigns, these collaborations can generate buzz and create a sense of community. Moreover, celebrity endorsements can add credibility and allure to your offerings, making them more appealing to potential buyers. It's essential to choose partners whose values align with yours to maintain authenticity and resonate with your audience.

Utilizing email marketing is a strategic way to keep your audience informed about new merchandise launches, exclusive sales, and promotions. Building an email list through your website and social media channels allows you to create targeted campaigns that reach your most engaged fans. Personalized emails that highlight product benefits, offer limited-time discounts, or share behind-the-scenes content can drive conversions and foster loyalty. Additionally, segmenting your email list based on buyer behavior enables you to tailor your messaging and promotions, further increasing the likelihood of sales.

25 Strategies, Tools, and Resources for Selling Merchandise Online and Promoting It

1. **Create a User-Friendly E-commerce Website**
   Why: A dedicated website for selling merchandise allows for full control over branding, design, and user experience. Your website acts as the central hub for all transactions and marketing efforts.

   Tool: Shopify or WooCommerce offer powerful e-commerce platforms that are easy to set up and manage, with built-in tools for inventory management and payment processing.

2. **Leverage Print-On-Demand Service**
   Why: Print-on-demand allows you to create and sell custom merchandise without holding inventory. Products are printed and shipped only when ordered, reducing upfront costs and risks.

   Tool: Printful or Teespring integrate with your e-commerce platform, allowing you to offer a wide range of customizable products like T-shirts, mugs, and phone cases.

3. **Use Social Media for Direct Sales**
   Why: Social media platforms like Instagram, Facebook, and Pinterest allow you to sell directly through integrated shopping

features. Social selling reaches customers where they spend their time online.

Tool: Instagram Shopping or Facebook Shops enable you to showcase products directly on your social media profiles and streamline the purchase process.

4. Run Paid Social Media Ads

Why: Paid ads on platforms like Instagram, Facebook, and Tik-Tok help target specific demographics, increasing visibility and driving traffic to your merchandise store. You can reach new customers who might not discover your products organically.

Tool: Facebook Ads Manager and TikTok Ads provide detailed targeting options to ensure your ads reach the right audience.

5. Offer Limited-Edition Products

Why: Limited-edition merchandise creates urgency and exclusivity, encouraging fans to purchase before the items are sold out. This strategy can increase sales while building a sense of community around your brand.

Tool: Use Countdown Timer tools like Hurrify to display the limited availability of your products and drive impulse purchases.

6. Collaborate with Influencers

Why: Partnering with influencers in your niche can increase brand visibility and credibility. Influencers can promote your merchandise to their engaged followers, driving traffic and sales.

Tool: Influencity or AspireIQ can help you identify and connect with influencers whose audience matches your target demographic.

7. Leverage Email Marketing

Why: Email marketing allows you to nurture your audience and promote new merchandise launches, discounts, and special offers. It's one of the most effective channels for driving repeat purchases.

Tool: Mailchimp or Klaviyo offer easy- to-use platforms for creating email campaigns, managing lists, and tracking results.

8. **Run Promotions and Discounts**

Why: Discounts and promotions incentivize purchases and help move inventory. You can run flash sales, offer discounts on bulk purchases, or provide free shipping to encourage conversions.

Tool: Use Shopify Discount Codes or WooCommerce Smart Coupons to create and manage promotions seamlessly.

9. **Create Bundled Merchandise Offers**

Why: Bundling products together at a discounted rate encourages customers to purchase more items in a single transaction, increasing the average order value.

Tool: Bold Bundles for Shopify allows you to create custom product bundles that offer savings for customers and increase your sales.

10. **Utilize Affiliate Marketing**

Why: Affiliate marketing allows others to promote your merchandise in exchange for a commission. Affiliates expand your reach and drive sales through their networks.

Tool: ShareASale or Rakuten Advertising provide platforms where you can recruit affiliates, track their performance, and pay commissions.

11. **Implement Retargeting Ads**

Why: Retargeting ads help you reach people who visited your store but didn't make a purchase. These ads remind potential customers about your products and can lead to conversions.

Tool: Google Display Network or Facebook Pixel are tools that allow you to set up retargeting campaigns to bring potential customers back to your store.

12. **Create Product Videos**
Why: Videos help showcase your merchandise in action and provide a more engaging experience than static images. Videos can explain product features, tell a story, or demonstrate use, making them more likely to convert viewers into buyers.

Tool: Animoto or Canva Video make it easy to create high-quality product videos for your website and social media.

13. **Leverage SEO for Organic Traffic**
Why: Search engine optimization (SEO) ensures that your merchandise store ranks well on search engines. Optimizing your website for relevant keywords can drive organic traffic without relying solely on paid ads.

Tool: Yoast SEO for Wordpress or Ahrefs can help you optimize your website content and analyze SEO performance to improve rankings.

14. **Use Customer Reviews and Testimonials**
Why: Social proof in the form of customer reviews and testimonials builds trust and credibility.

Displaying positive feedback on your product pages can increase conversions.

Tool: Yotpo or Judge.me allow you to collect and display customer reviews on your e-commerce site, improving your brand's reputation.

15. **Create Limited-Time Offers**

Why: Limited-time offers create a sense of urgency that encourages customers to act quickly. This strategy can increase sales and clear inventory during specific promotional periods.

Tool: Privy or Justuno offer tools to create and display limited-time offer popups and banners on your site.

16. **Implement an Abandoned Cart Recovery Strategy**

Why: Many customers abandon their carts before completing a purchase. An abandoned cart recovery strategy can help bring them back to finish the transaction.

Tool: Klaviyo or Shopify Abandoned Cart Recovery automatically send reminder emails to customers who have left items in their carts.

17. **Leverage User-Generated Content (UGC)**

Why: Encourage your customers to share photos and videos of themselves using your merchandise. UGC is powerful social proof and can be repurposed for marketing campaigns.

Tool: Pixlee or Taggbox help you collect, curate, and display UGC on your website and social media platforms.

18. **Offer Free Shipping**

Why: Free shipping is a major incentive for online shoppers and can increase conversion rates. If possible, offer free shipping for all orders or set a minimum purchase amount to qualify.

Tool: Shippo or ShipStation integrate with e-commerce platforms and help manage shipping logistics while offering competitive rates.

19. **Create a Loyalty Program**

Why: Loyalty programs encourage repeat purchases by rewarding customers with points, discounts, or exclusive products. This helps build a loyal customer base and increases customer life-time value.

Tool: Smile.io or LoyaltyLion allow you to set up and manage customer loyalty programs on your e- commerce site.

20. **Collaborate with Complementary Brands**
Why: Partnering with complementary brands can expand your reach and introduce your products to a new audience. Co- brand-ed merchandise or joint promotions can benefit both brands.

Tool: Collabfinder or Partnerize can help you find and manage collaborations with other brands.

21. **Use Pinterest for Visual Marketing**
Why: Pinterest is a visual search engine, making it a great plat-form for promoting merchandise. High- quality product pins can drive traffic to your website and increase sales.

Tool: Pinterest for Business provides analytics and promoted pin options to boost visibility and drive traffic to your store.

22. **Create Blog Content Around Your Merchandise**
Why: Blogging allows you to create content that highlights your merchandise in a way that adds value to your audience. Blog posts can provide styling tips, product tutorials, or the story behind your brand, driving traffic and engagement.

Tool: WordPress or Medium allow you to create and share blog content that can be optimized for SEO and promoted on social media.

23. **Host Virtual Events or Webinars**
Why: Virtual events, such as product launches or Q&A sessions, create excitement around your merchandise. These events offer

a more personal connection with your audience and allow for real-time interaction.

Tool: Zoom or Eventbrite can be used to host and promote virtual events that showcase your products.

24. **Create Engaging Social Media Content**
Why: Posting engaging content on social media helps build your brand and keep your audience engaged. Use a mix of product photos, videos, behind-the-scenes content, and customer stories to promote your merchandise.

Tool: Canva or Later help you create visually appealing posts and schedule content across multiple platforms.

25. **Use Analytics to Measure Success**
Why: Analyzing the performance of your marketing efforts is crucial for understanding what works and what doesn't. Data-driven decisions can help you optimize your campaigns for better results.

Tool: Google Analytics or Hotjar provide insights into visitor behavior, helping you track sales, conversion rates, and the effectiveness of your marketing efforts.

Conclusion

By leveraging these strategies, tools, and resources, you can build a successful online presence for selling merchandise and promoting it effectively. From social media marketing and email campaigns to user-generated content and partnerships, these approaches can help drive traffic, increase conversions, and build a loyal customer base for your brand.

Finally, incorporating analytics into your merchandise strategy is essential for ongoing success. Monitoring website traffic, conversion rates, and social media engagement can provide valuable insights into what resonates with your audience. Tools like Google Analytics and social media insights allow you to track performance metrics, helping you identify which products are popular and which marketing strategies yield the best results. By continuously assessing and adjusting your approach based on data, you can refine your merchandise offerings, optimize your marketing efforts, and ultimately drive greater sales in the competitive landscape of the entertainment industry.

Using Merchandise to Build Brand Loyalty

In the competitive landscape of the entertainment industry, building brand loyalty is essential for musicians, artists, filmmakers, influencers, and content creators.

Merchandise serves as a powerful tool in this endeavor, transforming casual fans into dedicated supporters. By strategically designing and marketing merchandise, creators can elevate their brand identity, foster a sense of community, and encourage repeat engagement. This subchapter explores how merchandise can be utilized to cultivate loyalty within your audience.

The first step in leveraging merchandise for brand loyalty is to ensure that the products resonate with your audience. This involves understanding your fan base's demographics, interests, and preferences. For musicians, this might mean offering items that reflect the themes of their music, such as apparel featuring album artwork or lyrics. Filmmakers could explore merchandise that connects with the stories they tell, like collectible items or behind-the-scenes content. By aligning merchandise with your brand's narrative, you create a deeper emotional connection with your audience, which is crucial for fostering loyalty.

Next, consider the quality and uniqueness of the merchandise you offer. In an era where consumers are inundated with options, high-quality, thoughtfully designed products stand out. This doesn't just mean the physical quality; the design should also reflect your brand's aesthetic and voice. Unique merchandise, such as limited-edition items or collaborations with other artists, can create a sense of exclusivity that fans crave. When fans feel that they own something special related to their favorite creator, their emotional investment in the brand increases, leading to stronger loyalty.

Moreover, merchandise can serve as a tangible representation of the community built around your brand. By offering items that encourage fan participation—such as custom-designed clothing for fans to wear at events, or collaboration opportunities for user-generated designs—you can foster a sense of belonging among your supporters. Social media campaigns that encourage fans to share their experiences with your merchandise can amplify this effect, creating a buzz around your brand and further solidifying fan loyalty. The more fans feel included in your brand's journey, the more likely they are to support it continuously.

Lastly, it's crucial to promote your merchandise effectively across all platforms. Utilize social media, email newsletters, and live events to showcase your products.

Engaging storytelling about the merchandise's significance can enhance its appeal. Consider integrating merchandise promotion into your overall marketing strategy, highlighting how fans can support you while also gaining something meaningful in return. By making the purchase process seamless and rewarding, you can transform one-time buyers into loyal brand advocates who are eager to share their experiences with others.

In conclusion, merchandise is not just a revenue stream; it is a vital element in building brand loyalty within the entertainment industry. By focusing on resonance, quality, community, and promotion, musicians, artists, filmmakers, and influencers can create a loyal fan base that extends beyond mere transactions. When fans feel connected to a brand, they are more likely to engage, share, and support it through various channels, ultimately leading to sustained success in their creative endeavors.

Chapter Twelve

Audience Engagement Tactics for Streaming Platforms

Understanding Your Audience's Preferences

Understanding your audience's preferences is a cornerstone of navigating the entertainment industry effectively. Musicians, artists, filmmakers, influencers, and content creators must grasp who their audience is, what they value, and how they engage with content. This knowledge not only informs your marketing strategies but also shapes your creative decisions, ensuring that your work resonates deeply with those you aim to reach. By prioritizing audience understanding, you can create authentic connections that enhance both your brand and your reach.

To begin, segmenting your audience is essential. Not all fans or followers are the same; they may differ in demographics, interests, and engagement levels. For instance, a musician might find that their audience consists of younger listeners who engage more on platforms like TikTok, while older fans might prefer Facebook or Instagram. Identifying these segments allows you to tailor your content accordingly. Utilize tools such as surveys, social media analytics, and audience insights to gather information that will help you create targeted campaigns that speak directly to each group's preferences.

Once you have a clear understanding of your audience segments, the next step is to analyze their consumption habits. This includes the types of content they prefer (videos, podcasts, behind-the-scenes footage, etc.), the platforms they use, and the times they are most active online. For example, filmmakers might discover that their target demographic engages more with short, impactful clips on social media rather than traditional trailers. By adapting your content strategy to align with these habits, you can increase engagement and drive interest in your projects, whether they be music releases, film launches, or influencer collaborations.

Engagement is not just about broadcasting your work; it's also about listening to your audience. Social media provides an invaluable avenue for interaction, allowing you to gather feedback on your content and understand what resonates. Pay attention to comments, direct messages, and shares to gauge audience sentiment. This feedback can inform not just future marketing campaigns but also the creative direction of your projects. Engaging with your audience fosters a sense of community, making them more likely to support your work through shares, attendance at events, and purchases.

Lastly, employing audience preferences in your marketing strategy can lead to more effective publicity efforts. When planning a promotional campaign, consider how your audience interacts with similar content and what types of messaging they respond to. Collaborations with relevant influencers or brands that align with your audience's interests can elevate your visibility. Additionally, utilizing data-driven insights to optimize your social media strategy ensures that your content reaches the right people at the right time. By continually adapting to your audience's preferences, you position yourself for sustained success in the ever- evolving entertainment landscape.

Interactive Content and Community Building

Interactive content has become an essential tool for musicians, artists, filmmakers, and influencers seeking to build a robust community around their work. In an age where audiences crave connection and engagement, simply sharing traditional content is no longer sufficient. By incorporating interactive elements—such as polls, quizzes, live Q&A sessions, and behind-the-scenes footage—creators can foster deeper relationships with their audiences. This not only enhances the overall experience for fans but also encourages them to become advocates for the creator's brand, driving word-of-mouth promotion and loyalty.

One of the most effective ways to leverage interactive content is through social media platforms that support real-time engagement. For instance, live streaming has gained immense popularity, allowing artists to connect with their followers in an immediate and personal manner. By hosting live performances, tutorials, or even casual chats, creators can invite their audience to participate actively, making them feel like part of the creative process. This sense of belonging can transform passive viewers into dedicated fans who are more likely to attend events, purchase merchandise, or share content with their own networks.

Community building extends beyond individual interactions; it involves creating spaces where fans can connect with one another. Online forums, dedicated social media groups, and fan clubs can facilitate discussions, sharing of fan art, and collaborative projects. By cultivating these environments, creators not only increase their reach but also empower their audience to take ownership of their fandom. This can lead to organic growth as engaged fans spread the word, share experiences, and contribute to a vibrant community that celebrates the creator's work.

Moreover, integrating interactive content into marketing strategies enhances brand partnerships and endorsements. Brands are increasingly looking for authentic connections with audiences, and interactive campaigns can provide measurable engagement metrics that demonstrate a creator's influence. For example, joint live events featuring both the artist and the brand can create dynamic experiences that resonate with fans. By showcasing these collaborations through interactive storytelling, creators can not only boost their visibility but also attract potential sponsors who see the value in engaging a dedicated community.

Finally, interactive content serves as a powerful tool for audience engagement on streaming platforms. By incorporating features like polls during watch parties or interactive storytelling elements in digital content, creators can enhance viewer participation and retention. This not only leads to a more immersive experience but also provides valuable insights into audience preferences and behaviors. As creators navigate the complexities of the entertainment industry, embracing interactive content and community building will be crucial for establishing a sustainable career and cultivating a loyal fan base.

Utilizing Feedback for Continuous Improvement

Feedback is a powerful tool for artists navigating the complex landscape of the entertainment industry. Whether you are a musician, filmmaker, influencer, or content creator, understanding how to utilize feedback effectively can enhance your work and refine your brand. Embracing feedback allows you to gain insights from diverse perspectives, helping you evolve creatively and strategically. Ultimately, the ability to interpret and act on feedback lays the groundwork for continuous improvement in your craft and career.

One of the first steps in utilizing feedback is to establish a feedback loop. This can involve soliciting opinions from trusted peers, mentors, and your audience. For musicians, this might mean sharing new tracks with fellow artists or engaging with fans through social media platforms.

Filmmakers can benefit from test screenings or pre- release viewings, where they can gather reactions and suggestions. Influencers and content creators should remain open to audience comments and critiques as they refine their content. By creating a structured process for gathering feedback, you can ensure that it becomes an integral part of your creative cycle, rather than an afterthought.

Analyzing feedback is just as crucial as collecting it. Not all feedback is created equal; some insights may resonate more deeply with your vision than others. It is essential to differentiate between constructive criticism and unfounded negativity. Look for patterns in the feedback you receive—if multiple sources echo the same sentiment, it may warrant further consideration. This analysis can guide your decision-making, whether you are adjusting your marketing strategy, refining your artistic direction, or deciding on collaborations. Focusing on actionable insights can transform feedback from mere commentary into a roadmap for growth.

Incorporating feedback into your work doesn't mean losing your unique voice. Instead, it allows you to enhance your authenticity by aligning your creations with your audience's expectations and preferences. For instance, musicians can use audience feedback on social media to inform their next album, ensuring it resonates with fans while staying true to their artistic identity.

Filmmakers can adjust narrative elements or marketing strategies based on viewer responses, leading to greater audience engagement. This balance of authenticity and responsiveness is vital for building a lasting brand in the entertainment industry.

Finally, remember that feedback is an ongoing process. The entertainment landscape is ever-evolving, and so are audience tastes and industry trends. Continuously seeking and integrating feedback ensures that you stay relevant and adaptable. By fostering a culture of openness to critique—both within your team and with your audience—you position yourself for sustained success. In this way, feedback becomes not just a tool for improvement, but a cornerstone of your brand strategy, allowing you to navigate the complexities of the entertainment industry with agility and confidence.

Chapter Thirteen

Content Marketing for Entertainment News and Reviews

Creating Valuable Content for Your Audience

Creating valuable content for your audience is essential for anyone navigating the entertainment industry, whether you're a musician, filmmaker, artist, influencer, or content creator. In a landscape saturated with options, the ability to produce relevant and engaging content can set you apart from the competition. Valuable content not only showcases your artistry but also establishes a connection with your audience, making them more likely to support your work and share it with others.

Understanding your audience is the first step in crafting valuable content. Conducting thorough research can help you identify their interests, preferences, and pain points. Utilize social media analytics, surveys, and feedback to gather insights about what resonates with your followers. For musicians, this might mean exploring what types of music videos or behind-the-scenes content engage fans the most. For filmmakers, it could involve finding out what aspects of production or storytelling captivate viewers. Tailoring your content to reflect these insights ensures that you are meeting the needs of your audience while showcasing your unique voice.

The format of your content plays a crucial role in its value. Different platforms cater to various types of media, from short videos on TikTok to in-depth articles on blogs.

Experimenting with different formats can help you determine what works best for your audience. For instance, musicians might find success in creating engaging live streams or interactive Q&A sessions, while filmmakers could benefit from sharing teaser trailers or behind-the-scenes footage. Additionally, consider incorporating user-generated content, which not only fosters community but also provides fresh perspectives that can enhance your narrative.

Consistency is another vital component in creating valuable content. Establishing a regular posting schedule helps to build anticipation among your audience and keeps them engaged. By committing to a content calendar, you can strategically plan releases around important dates, such as album launches, film premieres, or social media campaigns. Consistency does not mean sacrificing quality; rather, it involves finding a balance that allows you to produce authentic, high- quality content on a reliable basis. This approach cultivates trust and loyalty, as your audience learns to expect and look forward to your contributions.

Lastly, always prioritize authenticity and storytelling in your content. Audiences are drawn to genuine narratives that resonate on a personal level. Sharing your journey, including both successes and challenges, can create a deeper connection with your audience. Whether you are an artist discussing your creative process or a filmmaker sharing the inspiration behind your latest project, storytelling humanizes your brand and invites your audience to engage with your work on a more meaningful level. By focusing on authenticity and value, you can create content that not only enhances your visibility but also fosters a loyal and engaged community around your brand.

Leveraging SEO for Visibility

Leveraging SEO for visibility is an essential strategy for musicians, artists, filmmakers, influencers, and content creators seeking to carve out a niche in the competitive landscape of the entertainment industry. Search Engine Optimization (SEO) is a fundamental digital marketing technique that enhances the visibility of your content across various online platforms. By optimizing your website, social media profiles, and digital content, you can significantly increase your chances of being discovered by potential fans, collaborators, and industry professionals. For those in the entertainment sector, where competition is fierce, implementing effective SEO strategies can make a notable difference in career trajectories.

One of the first steps in leveraging SEO is keyword research. This process involves identifying the terms and phrases your target audience is using to search for content related to your work. For musicians, this might include genre-specific terms, song titles, or even lyrics. Filmmakers might focus on keywords related to their film's themes, cast, or genre. By understanding and incorporating these keywords into your website and content, you can enhance your chances of appearing in search engine results when potential fans or industry professionals are looking for similar content. Tools like Google Keyword Planner, SEMrush, or Ahrefs can assist in uncovering relevant keywords that align with your audience's search behavior.

Once you have identified your keywords, it's crucial to integrate them effectively into your online presence. This means incorporating them into your website's metadata, such as titles, descriptions, and image alt texts, as well as using them naturally within your blog posts, music descriptions, or film synopses. For content creators, maintaining a blog or a news section on your website can be a powerful way to engage audiences while optimizing for SEO. By routinely publishing content that features relevant keywords, you not only enhance your site's searchability but also establish yourself as an authority in your niche, whether it's music, film, or influencer marketing.

Additionally, building backlinks is a critical component of successful SEO. Backlinks are links from other websites that direct traffic to your site, signaling to search engines that your content is credible and valuable. Collaborating with other artists, bloggers, or influencers for guest posts, interviews, or features can create opportunities for backlinks. This strategy not only boosts your SEO but also helps you reach new audiences. Participating in industry forums, engaging with online communities, and sharing your insights can further enhance your visibility, as others will link back to your work when referencing your expertise or contributions.

Finally, monitoring and adapting your SEO strategies is vital for ongoing success. Utilizing analytics tools to track your website's performance, visitor behavior, and keyword rankings will provide valuable insights into what works and what doesn't. The digital landscape is constantly evolving, and staying informed about changes in search engine algorithms and audience preferences is essential. By regularly refining your SEO tactics, you can ensure that your content remains visible and relevant, ultimately aiding in your quest for fame and recognition in the entertainment industry. Embracing SEO isn't just a technical requirement; it's a powerful tool that can elevate your brand and enhance your connection with your audience.

Building a Network of Content Collaborators

Building a network of content collaborators is a crucial step for musicians, artists, filmmakers, influencers, and content creators looking to thrive in the competitive landscape of the entertainment industry. As you navigate this multifaceted environment, the ability to connect with like-minded individuals and organizations can amplify your reach and enhance your brand's visibility.

Collaborators can range from fellow creators to brands seeking partnerships, and each relationship can open doors to new audiences and opportunities.

To start building your network, focus on identifying potential collaborators who align with your artistic vision and values. This could include other musicians, filmmakers, or influencers whose work resonates with your own. Attend industry events, workshops, and networking gatherings where you can meet these individuals face-to-face. Online platforms, such as social media and professional networks, are also invaluable for initiating relationships. Engaging with their content, sharing their work, and participating in discussions can help you establish rapport before reaching out with collaboration proposals.

Once you've identified potential collaborators, it's important to approach them with a clear value proposition. Articulate how a partnership could be mutually beneficial. For instance, if you're a musician looking to team up with a filmmaker, you might highlight how your music can enhance their visual storytelling, while their film could provide exposure to your music. Being specific about how the collaboration can serve both parties will increase the likelihood of a positive response. Additionally, be open to exploring various formats of collaboration, such as co-hosting events, joint social media campaigns, or cross-promotional content.

Collaboration can also extend beyond individual creators to include brands and organizations that resonate with your brand identity. Partnering with brands for endorsements or sponsorships can not only provide financial support but also lend credibility to your work. When approaching brands, present them with a well-thought-out proposal that outlines your audience demographics, engagement metrics, and how their values align with your content. This strategic approach will demonstrate the potential for a successful partnership that benefits both parties.

Finally, nurturing these relationships is key to building a robust network. Regularly check in with your collaborators, share updates on your projects, and celebrate their successes as well. Consider creating a dedicated space for collaboration, such as a group chat or a shared project management tool, where you can brainstorm ideas and keep communication lines open. By fostering a collaborative spirit and maintaining strong connections, you can create a dynamic network that not only enhances your visibility but also enriches your creative journey within the entertainment industry.

Chapter Fourteen

Conclusion and Next Steps

Recap of Key Strategies

In the rapidly evolving landscape of the entertainment industry, musicians, artists, filmmakers, influencers, and content creators must equip themselves with effective strategies to stand out and thrive. This subchapter serves as a recap of key strategies outlined throughout the book "DIY Fame: Navigating the Entertainment Industry Without a Publicist." By synthesizing these strategies, readers can develop a comprehensive plan to enhance their visibility and engagement across various platforms.

One of the foundational strategies discussed is the importance of establishing a strong personal brand. This involves creating a unique identity that resonates with your target audience. Musicians and artists should focus on developing a cohesive visual and narrative style that reflects their values and artistic vision. Filmmakers and content creators can benefit from crafting a consistent message that aligns with the themes of their projects. By leveraging social media platforms, creators can communicate their brand story effectively, fostering a connection with their audience that extends beyond their work.

Another critical aspect of navigating the entertainment industry is mastering digital marketing strategies. The chapter emphasizes the significance of utilizing social media analytics and audience insights to tailor marketing campaigns. For indie filmmakers and musicians, understanding which platforms yield the highest engagement can inform decisions about where to focus promotional efforts. Additionally, crafting compelling content marketing strategies, such as behind-the-scenes glimpses or interactive Q&A sessions, can enhance audience engagement and build anticipation for upcoming releases.

Influencer marketing emerges as a vital tactic for creators looking to amplify their reach. Collaborating with influencers who align with their brand can provide access to new audiences and foster credibility. This strategy is particularly relevant in the music industry, where artists can partner with influencers to promote new singles or albums through curated content. Similarly, filmmakers can engage influencers to drive interest in film premieres or festivals, leveraging their established followings to create buzz and excitement around their projects.

Event marketing also plays a crucial role in promoting films and music. Organizing premiere events or participating in industry festivals can significantly elevate a creator's profile. The recap highlights the importance of strategic partnerships with brands for event sponsorships and collaborations. Such partnerships can enhance the event experience while providing additional promotional channels. By integrating merchandise branding and audience engagement tactics into these events, creators can create memorable experiences that resonate with attendees and encourage them to become advocates for their work.

In sum, the strategies discussed in this chapter serve as a roadmap for navigating the complexities of the entertainment industry. By focusing on personal branding, digital marketing, influencer collaborations, and event marketing, musicians, artists, filmmakers, and content creators can effectively carve out their niche. As they implement these strategies, they will not only enhance their visibility but also foster lasting connections with their audiences, paving the way for sustainable success in an increasingly competitive landscape.

Creating Your DIY Fame Action Plan

Creating a DIY Fame Action Plan requires a strategic approach tailored to your unique strengths and the specific niches within the entertainment industry. The first step is to define your brand identity. This involves a thorough self-assessment to understand what sets you apart from others in your field. Musicians may focus on their sound and image, while filmmakers might highlight their storytelling style or visual aesthetics.

Influencers and content creators should consider their niche and the type of audience they attract. Establishing a clear brand vision will guide your marketing efforts and ensure consistency across all platforms and promotional materials.

Next, outline your goals and objectives. What do you hope to achieve with your DIY fame strategy? Goals could range from increasing your social media following and gaining media coverage to securing collaborations with other artists or brands. Be specific and set measurable targets to track your progress. For instance, if your aim is to enhance your online presence, you might set a goal to grow your Instagram following by 30% over six months or to secure three interviews with industry-related podcasts. By having concrete objectives, you can create actionable steps that lead you closer to your vision of fame.

Developing a comprehensive marketing strategy is crucial for executing your action plan. This strategy should encompass various channels, including social media, press outreach, and event participation. Identify which platforms resonate most with your target audience and focus your efforts there. For musicians, platforms like TikTok and Spotify can be vital for music discovery, while filmmakers may benefit from showcasing their work on Vimeo or YouTube. Use content marketing techniques to tell your story and engage your audience, employing visuals, behind-the-scenes footage, and personal anecdotes that align with your brand identity.

Networking and building relationships within the industry is another essential component of your DIY fame action plan. Connecting with fellow artists, influencers, and industry professionals can open doors to collaboration opportunities, endorsements, and partnerships. Attend industry events, film festivals, and music showcases to establish face-to-face connections. Utilize social media to engage with others in your niche, share their content, and participate in conversations. Consider reaching out to potential collaborators or mentors through direct messaging or email, but always approach these interactions with authenticity and respect.

Lastly, continuously evaluate and adjust your action plan based on feedback and results. Monitor your social media engagement, website traffic, and any media coverage you receive. Analyze which strategies yield the best results and be open to pivoting your approach when necessary. Audience engagement tactics, such as polls and Q&A sessions, can provide valuable insights into what resonates with your followers. By remaining adaptable and committed to your goals, you can refine your DIY fame action plan and navigate the entertainment industry with confidence and creativity.

Staying Adaptable in a Changing Industry

Staying adaptable in a rapidly changing entertainment industry is crucial for musicians, artists, filmmakers, influencers, and content creators. The landscape is continually evolving, influenced by technological advancements, shifting audience preferences, and new social media trends. To thrive without the traditional support of a publicist, individuals must cultivate an agile mindset that embraces change and encourages innovation. This adaptability not only enhances personal branding but also opens doors to unique opportunities that may not have been previously considered.

One of the key components of adaptability is staying informed about industry trends and emerging technologies. For instance, the rise of streaming platforms has fundamentally altered how content is distributed and consumed. Musicians and filmmakers must familiarize themselves with these platforms' algorithms to optimize visibility and engagement.

Understanding the nuances of digital marketing strategies can empower creators to effectively reach their target audiences. Subscribing to industry newsletters, attending webinars, and participating in online communities can provide insights into what strategies are working and where the industry is headed.

Networking and collaboration also play essential roles in adaptability. The entertainment industry thrives on relationships, and building a diverse network can introduce creators to new ideas and partnerships. Collaborating with other artists, brands, or influencers can lead to innovative projects that resonate with audiences in fresh ways.

Additionally, engaging with peers through social media can provide real-time feedback and support, helping creators to pivot their strategies as needed. Being open to collaboration and fostering a spirit of community can yield unexpected benefits and strengthen one's presence in the industry.

Another aspect of staying adaptable is embracing feedback and learning from failures. The entertainment industry is often unpredictable, and not every project will achieve the desired outcome. Instead of viewing setbacks as failures, creators should see them as valuable learning experiences. Analyzing what went wrong and seeking constructive criticism can lead to improvements in future endeavors. This resilience and willingness to evolve are essential for long-term success, allowing artists and creators to refine their approach and better cater to their audience's needs.

Finally, maintaining a strong personal brand is vital in a changing industry. The ability to pivot and adapt while staying true to one's artistic vision can create a unique identity that resonates with audiences. By consistently producing quality content, engaging with fans, and being authentic in their messaging, creators can build a loyal following that will support them through industry fluctuations. In an environment where trends come and go, a solid personal brand serves as a foundation for navigating the complexities of the entertainment landscape, ensuring that artists remain relevant and influential in their respective fields.

50 Tips for Unlocking the Secrets to Self-Promotion and Industry Success: Your Blueprint for Independent Stardom in the Entertainment World

1. **Define Your Unique Value Proposition (UVP)**
   Know what sets you apart from others. Highlight your strengths, talents, and the unique angle you bring to your craft. This will help you stand out in a crowded industry.

2. **Create a Strong Personal Brand**
   Develop a consistent image, tone, and style across all platforms. Your personal brand should reflect who you are and the message you want to convey to your audience.

3. **Leverage Social Media**
   Establish a strong presence on platforms like Instagram, Twitter, TikTok, and Facebook. Engage regularly with your audience by posting content that resonates with your brand and attracts followers.

4. **Design a Professional Website**
   Create a personal website that serves as your digital portfo-

lio. Include your bio, reel, resume, press mentions, and contact information. A well-designed site makes you look polished and professional.

5. **Develop a Content Strategy**

Plan a consistent content calendar for your social media and website. Post regularly to keep your audience engaged, and mix up your content with photos, videos, and behind-the-scenes stories.

6. **Create High-Quality Visuals**

Invest in professional photography, cover art, or graphic design for your promotional materials. High-quality visuals elevate your brand and make you more memorable.

7. **Be Authentic**

Authenticity builds trust with your audience. Share your real self, including your successes and challenges, to form a deeper connection with your followers.

8. **Network with Industry Peers**

Build relationships with other creatives, industry professionals, and influencers. Networking is key to opening doors, getting referrals, and collaborating on projects.

9. **Create a Consistent Brand Voice**

Your voice should be consistent across all platforms. Whether you're humorous, inspirational, or edgy, your audience should always recognize your unique tone.

10. **Maintain a Positive Public Image**

Be mindful of how you present yourself both online and offline. Avoid controversial or negative behavior that could harm your reputation.

11. **Engaging with Your Audience**

Respond to comments, messages, and interactions from your

followers. Building relationships with your fans fosters loyalty and increases engagement.

12. Host Live Q&A Sessions

Use platforms like Instagram Live, YouTube, or Twitch to connect with your audience in real-time. Live sessions offer a personal connection and allow fans to engage with you directly.

13. Create User-Generated Content Campaigns

Encourage your fans to create content related to your work, such as fan art, covers, or remixes. Share their contributions to build a community around your brand.

14. Offer Behind-the-Scenes Content

Show your audience what goes on behind the scenes of your projects. Sharing your creative process makes your journey more relatable and human.

15. Provide Exclusive Content

Reward your most dedicated followers with exclusive content like early releases, backstage passes, or members-only newsletters. Platforms like Patreon allow you to monetize this content.

16. Start an Email Newsletter

Collect email addresses from your fans and send regular updates. Newsletters allow you to connect more personally and keep your audience informed about upcoming releases or events.

17. Offer Freebies or Giveaways

Giveaways create excitement and engagement. Offer free merch, exclusive content, or tickets to events to incentivize participation and attract new followers.

18. Share Your Story

People connect with stories. Share your journey, struggles, and triumphs with your audience to create an emotional connection.

19. Use Polls and Surveys

Engage your audience with polls and surveys to get their input on upcoming projects or ideas. This interaction makes your fans feel involved in your creative process.

20. Recognize Your Top Supporters

Shout out your most dedicated fans, whether through social media posts or special thank-yous in your content. Recognition encourages continued support.

21. Collaborate with Other Creators

Partner with other artists, filmmakers, or influencers for joint projects.

Collaborations expand your reach and introduce you to new audiences.

22. Attend Industry Events

Film festivals, music conferences, and networking events offer valuable opportunities to meet industry professionals and showcase your work. Don't be shy about introducing yourself and making connections.

23. Join Professional Organizations

Becoming a member of industry organizations can give you access to networking events, workshops, and resources that can help boost your career.

24. Reach Out to Influencers

Collaborating with influencers who align with your brand can amplify your reach. Influencers can promote your work to their dedicated followers.

25. Build Relationships with Journalists and Bloggers

Cultivate relationships with media professionals who cover your industry. Positive press coverage can increase your visibility and credibility.

26. **Pitch Your Story to the Media**

    Craft compelling press releases and pitch your story to relevant outlets. Getting featured in publications, blogs, or podcasts can expand your reach and attract new fans.

27. **Use LinkedIn for Professional Networking**

    LinkedIn is an excellent platform for connecting with industry professionals and building your network. Join relevant groups and engage with content in your industry to raise your profile.

28. **Work with a Publicist (When Ready)**

    Hiring a publicist can help secure media coverage, manage your image, and elevate your profile. Publicists often have relationships with key players in the industry.

29. **Use Crowdfunding for Projects**

    Crowdfunding platforms like Kickstarter or Indiegogo allow you to raise money while building a community around your project. Successfully funded projects often attract industry attention.

30. **Get Involved in Industry Panels or Speaking Engagements**

    Sharing your knowledge and experience on panels or as a guest speaker can establish you as an authority in your field, leading to more opportunities and exposure.

31. **Use Analytics to Track Your Progress**

    Analytics tools can help you understand your audience's behavior, allowing you to optimize your content strategy. Platforms like Google Analytics or social media insights provide valuable data.

32. **Invest in Digital Marketing**

    Paid ads on Google, Facebook, or Instagram can boost your visibility and target specific audiences. Digital marketing can help drive traffic to your content or events.

33. **Optimize Your Content for SEO**

    Search engine optimization (SEO) ensures that your website and content rank higher on search engines like Google. Optimizing for SEO can increase organic traffic to your site.

34. **Build a Strong YouTube Presence**
YouTube is the second-largest search engine, making it a powerful platform for sharing your content. Optimize your videos with catchy titles, descriptions, and tags to increase visibility.

35. **Create Engaging Thumbnails for Videos**
Eye-catching thumbnails can make the difference between someone clicking on your video or passing it by. Use engaging visuals that represent your brand.

36. **Run Social Media Contests**
Contests can boost engagement and attract new followers. Encourage your audience to participate by offering attractive prizes and promoting the contest across platforms.

37. **Use Scheduling Tools to Stay Consistent**
Consistency is key to maintaining an online presence. Use scheduling tools like Buffer or Later to plan and automate your social media posts.

38. **Leverage Podcast Appearances**
Appearing as a guest on podcasts allows you to share your story with a new audience. Reach out to podcast hosts in your niche and pitch yourself as a guest.

39. **Build a Spotify Presence (For Musicians)**
Spotify is a powerful platform for musicians. Optimize your artist profile, submit your music to playlists, and engage with fans through Spotify for Artists.

40. **Create Shareable Content**
Memes, gifs, and bite-sized content are highly shareable and can quickly increase your visibility. Create content that your audience will want to share with their networks.

41. **Stay Persistent and Resilient**

The entertainment industry is tough, and rejection is part of the journey. Stay persistent, keep improving your craft, and don't let setbacks discourage you.

42. **Set Clear Goals**

Define your short-term and long-term goals, both professionally and creatively. Clear goals keep you focused and help you track your progress.

43. **Keep Learning**

Continuously educate yourself through workshops, online courses, and industry news. Staying current with trends and skills ensures you remain competitive.

44. **Surround Yourself with Positive Influences**

Build a supportive network of peers and mentors who uplift and challenge you. Having a positive environment can keep you motivated and inspired.

45. **Be Adaptable**

The industry is constantly evolving, and you need to be flexible and willing to adapt. Embrace change and be open to exploring new trends and technologies.

46. **Take Risks**

Success often comes from stepping out of your comfort zone. Take calculated risks with your projects, collaborations, and promotional strategies.

47. **Stay Organized**

Keep track of your projects, deadlines, and promotional efforts with tools like Trello, Asana, or Google Calendar. Staying organized helps you balance your creative work with self-promotion.

48. **Practice Self-Care**

Building a career in entertainment can be demanding. Make time for self-care to avoid burnout and maintain your mental and physical well-being.

49. **Stay Consistent with Your Efforts**

Success doesn't happen overnight. Consistency in your work, promotion, and engagement will build momentum and lead to long-term success.

50. **Celebrate Small Wins**

Recognize and celebrate your achievements, no matter how small. Celebrating milestones boosts your confidence and reminds you of how far you've come on your journey to stardom.

Conclusion

Achieving independent stardom in the entertainment industry requires a mix of strategic self-promotion, consistent effort, and networking. These 50 tips provide a comprehensive blueprint to help you navigate the complexities of the industry, build a loyal fanbase, and elevate your career. Stay focused, keep growing, and embrace the journey ahead!

Chapter Fifteen

Summary

In the modern entertainment industry, success increasingly relies on creators taking control of their personal branding and self-promotion. DIY fame allows artists, musicians, filmmakers, and other creatives to navigate their careers without relying on a traditional publicist. Building a strong brand and identity is the cornerstone of this approach. By defining a unique value proposition, creating consistent and engaging content, and leveraging social media platforms, creators can establish their presence in the industry. Authenticity, visual appeal, and regular audience engagement are key to forming connections with fans and standing out in a crowded market. Networking and collaboration further extend reach, opening doors to new opportunities and growth.

DIY Fame: Navigating the Entertainment Industry Without a Publicist

Navigating the entertainment industry without a publicist requires a proactive and strategic approach to building your brand and identity. By utilizing the right tools, cultivating an authentic presence, and continuously engaging with your audience, you can create lasting connections that drive your career forward. Embracing the DIY mentality empowers you to take control of your destiny in the entertainment world, positioning yourself for long-term success while maintaining creative freedom.

25 Case Studies

1. **Lil Nas X**

   Background: Lil Nas X rose to fame with his viral hit "Old Town Road," which he promoted primarily through TikTok. He leveraged meme culture, engaged with his followers on Twitter, and built a strong personal brand that resonated with diverse audiences.

   Key Strategies: TikTok virality, meme marketing, and consistent social media engagement.

2. **Issa Rae**

   Background: Issa Rae started as a YouTuber with her series *The Misadventures of Awkward Black Girl*. She used social media to build a fanbase and later transitioned to HBO with her hit show Insecure.

   Key Strategies: YouTube content creation, direct fan engagement, and leveraging her personal experiences.

3. **Chance the Rapper**

   Background: Chance the Rapper famously rejected record labels to remain independent. He used platforms like SoundCloud to distribute his music for free and built his brand through live performances and social media.

   Key Strategies: Free music distribution, fan interaction on social media, and community engagement.

4. Bo Burnham

Background: Bo Burnham started his career by posting comedic songs on YouTube. He self-promoted his work and built a large following, which led to comedy specials on major platforms.

Key Strategies: YouTube self-promotion, organic social media growth, and content creation.

5. Halsey

Background: Halsey released her music independently on platforms like SoundCloud before signing with a major label. She cultivated a strong online presence and connected deeply with fans through social media.

Key Strategies: Independent music release, authentic social media engagement, and storytelling.

6. Tyler, The Creator

Background: Tyler, The Creator and his collective Odd Future used social media and blogs to build a grassroots following. They created their own music, merchandise, and videos, bypassing traditional industry structures.

Key Strategies: DIY branding, independent content creation, and social media engagement.

7. Rupi Kaur

Background: Rupi Kaur built her career as a poet by sharing her work on Instagram. She self-published her poetry and used social media to build a massive following, leading to mainstream success.

Key Strategies: Instagram poetry, self-publishing, and community engagement.

8. **Cardi B**

Background: Cardi B gained fame through her candid personality and viral videos on Vine and Instagram. She used her social media presence to promote her music and build a loyal fanbase before breaking into mainstream success.

Key Strategies: Social media presence, viral video content, and personal branding.

9. **Troye Sivan**

Background: Troye Sivan began as a YouTuber, posting vlogs and music covers. He self-promoted his content across multiple platforms, leading to a successful music and acting career.

Key Strategies: YouTube vlogging, cross-platform promotion, and consistent fan engagement.

10. **Lilly Singh**

Background: Lilly Singh, also known as Superwoman, built her brand on YouTube by creating comedic skits and relatable content. She used social media to grow her following, eventually leading to her own late-night talk show.

Key Strategies: YouTube content creation, social media engagement, and relatable storytelling.

11. **Donald Glover (Childish Gambino)**

Background: Donald Glover, also known as Childish Gambino, self-promoted his music and acting career through social media and online platforms. He built a unique brand that spanned multiple creative industries.

Key Strategies: Cross-platform branding, social media promotion, and multi-talented content creation.

12. **Tessa Violet**

Background: Tessa Violet transitioned from being a YouTuber to an indie music artist by promoting her music directly to her YouTube fanbase. She continues to leverage social media and YouTube to promote her work independently.

Key Strategies: YouTube promotion, social media engagement, and direct fan interaction.

13. **Brittany Broski**

Background: Brittany Broski, also known as "Kombucha Girl," gained viral fame through TikTok. She leveraged her newfound fame to build a strong online presence and transitioned into acting and hosting gigs.

Key Strategies: TikTok virality, meme marketing, and brand partnerships.

14. **Shane Dawson**

Background: Shane Dawson built his career on YouTube by creating comedy sketches, conspiracy theory videos, and documentaries. He used his platform to promote his own projects, such as books and makeup collaborations.

Key Strategies: YouTube content creation, self-promotion, and cross-industry branding.

15. **Amanda Palmer**

Background: Musician Amanda Palmer has successfully used crowdfunding platforms like Kickstarter and Patreon to finance her music independently. She built a direct relationship with her fans, bypassing traditional industry channels.

Key Strategies: Crowdfunding, fan engagement, and direct-to-fan marketing.

16. **Jacob Collier**

Background: Jacob Collier is a multi- instrumentalist and composer who gained recognition through YouTube. He built a loyal fanbase by sharing his music and process online, eventually winning multiple Grammy Awards.

Key Strategies: YouTube music promotion, educational content, and global fan engagement.

17. **Clairo**

Background: Clairo gained fame after her DIY music video for "Pretty Girl" went viral on YouTube. She used social media to build a following and eventually secured record deals, but continues to promote her music independently.

Key Strategies: YouTube virality, self- promotion on social media, and indie music distribution.

18. **Awkwafina**

Background: Awkwafina began her career by releasing comedic rap videos on YouTube. She built her personal brand through self-promotion and networking, eventually transitioning into acting with major roles in films like *Crazy Rich Asians*.

Key Strategies: YouTube music promotion, social media branding, and cross-industry networking.

19. **Yungblud**

Background: Yungblud used social media and touring to build a strong fanbase. He actively engages with his fans on platforms like Instagram and Twitter, promoting his music and merchandise without relying heavily on traditional PR strategies.

Key Strategies: Social media fan engagement, DIY touring, and merchandise promotion.

20. **Bhad Bhabie**

Background: Bhad Bhabie, also known as Danielle Bregoli, rose to fame through a viral moment on Dr. Phil. She capitalized on her newfound fame through social media and self-promotion, transitioning into a successful music career.

Key Strategies: Viral marketing, social media branding, and direct fan engagement.

21. **Joji**

Background: Joji, formerly known as Filthy Frank on YouTube, transitioned from comedy videos to a music career. He leveraged his existing fanbase and YouTube platform to promote his music independently before signing with a label.

Key Strategies: YouTube promotion, cross- platform content, and independent music distribution.

22. **Hobo Johnson**

Background: Hobo Johnson gained fame through viral Facebook videos that showcased his unique blend of spoken word and music. He used social media to connect with fans and promote his music independently.

Key Strategies: Viral video marketing, social media engagement, and direct fan interaction.

23. **Liza Koshy**

Background: Liza Koshy built her brand on Vine and YouTube through comedic skits. She transitioned her online success into acting roles, hosting gigs, and brand partnerships by leveraging her massive social media following.

Key Strategies: Social media branding, content creation, and cross-platform promotion.

24. **Russ**

Background: Russ is a rapper and producer who built his career independently by releasing a new song every week on Sound-Cloud. He used social media to promote his music and connect with fans, eventually gaining mainstream success.

Key Strategies: Consistent music release, social media engagement, and fan-driven promotion.

25. **Rachel Bloom**

Background: Rachel Bloom gained attention through her viral comedy music videos on YouTube, which led to her successful TV show *Crazy Ex-Girlfriend*.

She used social media and online platforms to build a loyal fanbase before breaking into mainstream television.

Key Strategies: YouTube comedy content, social media engagement, and DIY branding.

Conclusion

These 25 case studies demonstrate that self- promotion, social media engagement, and strong branding can lead to significant success in the entertainment industry. By leveraging digital platforms, building a loyal fanbase, and maintaining control over their creative output, these celebrities have achieved fame and success without relying heavily on traditional PR methods. The DIY approach is becoming increasingly viable, offering creators new opportunities to break into the industry on their own terms.

www.ingramcontent.com/pod-product-compliance
Lightning Source LLC
Chambersburg PA
CBHW071752120626
46550CB00002B/760